MW00974382

LASTING
IMPRESSIONS
A Medium's Cherished Messages from Spirit

GEOFFREY JOWETT

LASTING IMPRESSIONS
A MEDIUM'S CHERISHED MESSAGES FROM SPIRIT

iUniverse books may be ordered through booksellers or by contacting:

iUniverse
1663 Liberty Drive
Bloomington, IN 47403
www.iuniverse.com
1-800-Authors (1-800-288-4677)

ISBN: 978-1-5320-3727-6 (sc)
ISBN: 978-1-5320-3728-3 (hc)
ISBN: 978-1-5320-3726-9 (e)

Library of Congress Control Number: 2017919518

Print information available on the last page.

iUniverse rev. date: 01/05/2018

"Lasting Impressions by Geof Jowett has been brilliantly crafted to teach us about four vitally important aspects of spirit communication. With fearless honesty, he teaches us what it's like to be a medium. With sincere compassion, he teaches us how to be better clients. With deep respect, he teaches us the wants and needs of spirits. And with admirable analysis and introspection, Geof teaches us the purpose of mediumship based on his experiences. This is an unforgettable, eye-opening contribution to understanding spirit communication from a medium's perspective."

Bob Olson
Author of *Answers About the Afterlife, The Magic Mala* and host of AfterlifeTV.com

*   *   *

"Your instincts may have 'coincidentally' led you to check out this book if you are on a path of discovering more about yourself and your place in the universe."

"'On earth as it is in heaven' is part of a prayer suggesting we are eternally connected to the Source and thus to 'all that is.' Science, through the study of quantum physics, is bringing us closer and closer to this spiritual truth.

This book will give you touching insights into one part of that cosmic dance: the relationship between the spirit world (including pets and signs from nature), you who seek to connect, and the medium who facilitates the connection.

Especially insightful for me were the illustrations of 'on earth and in heaven.' The expressions of love, and sometimes forgiveness, from our 'soul family' in the spirit world can be very healing for those of us here on earth. But equally helpful and healing are the love, understanding, and sometimes forgiveness that we project to those continuing their spiritual journey in heaven."

Neal Rzepkowski, MD
Registered medium and 2017/18 president of the Lily Dale Assembly, the international center for spiritualism, Lily Dale, NY

*   *   *

"Jowett is a healer, mystic, and altogether a wonderful spiritual teacher. Science and Spirit mix beautifully with him."

James Van Praagh
Author of NYT bestseller *Talking to Heaven*

Cherish is the word I use to describe
All the feeling that I have hiding here for you inside
You don't know how many times I've wished that I had told you
You don't know how many times I've wished that I could hold you
You don't know how many times I've wished that I could mold you
Into someone who could cherish me as much as I cherish you.

"Cherish" ~ The Association

DEDICATION

This book is devoted to all those we love in the spirit world, with gratitude for their kind encouragement, inspiring wisdom, and deep compassion, and their continual reminders that we are never apart and we are always loved.

ACKNOWLEDGMENTS

With appreciation for . . .

All those clients who entrust me with presenting their cherished messages from their loved ones in the spirit world.

Dawn Pfeufer, medium and spiritual artist, for creatively designing the images within this book.

Peggy Henrikson, for devoting her heart and soul to the editing of the book. Peggy's expertise in the mechanics of writing and editing plus her enthusiasm for the book's subject and extensive background in spirituality were a karmic match for *Lasting Impressions*.

CONTENTS

PART 4: THE SPIRIT

PART 5: THE MESSAGE

PART 1
MEDIUMSHIP

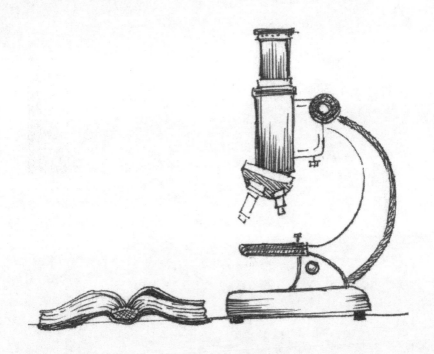

MY BACKGROUND AS A SCIENTIFIC MEDIUM

"Science is not only compatible with spirituality;
it is a profound source of spirituality."
~ Carl Sagan

Spirits are genuine and real! My earliest memories are of waking up, holding the rails of my crib, and staring with awe and wonder at the reflection of four luminescent entities in my window. They had a translucent radiance, unlike my stuffed animals, and they were more soft-spoken than my sisters. I found it fascinating that I was able to hear them in my mind and feel them intensely in my heart, even though their lips didn't move.

These light beings impressed into my psyche a dimension not known to others, a world of mystical light, tender kindness, and higher understanding. In their presence, I felt their sweetness, like that of my caring grandma, and a sense of safety and security as soft as my warm blanky. I was bewildered that no one else saw these affectionately caring and sensible spirits.

As a kid, I didn't know what to think about these light beings because none of my friends ever mentioned similar sightings. I preferred to spent lots of time alone (or so others thought) and had unpredictable visits by gentle but stimulating spirits. They taught me about an exhilarating plane of existence that parallels the earth plane and is the home of the spirit when it ends its brief visit to this planet.

3

Lovingly, my spirits telepathically taught me about the soul. They explained the value of temporarily visiting the vivid, dramatic, and emotional earth plane and the progression of beliefs and feelings. They taught me about karma, and the initiation and awakening to higher levels of consciousness. The earth plane, they said, is a place for our spirits to experiment, research, and investigate the limitless dimensions of truth so we can remember our sacred and divine nature.

To better know the meaning of life, I decided to explore the notion of death. In my childhood, I collected dead animals, had funerals for them, and buried them in a makeshift pet cemetery. I sought to determine where the dead animals' soul life force went. Digging up carcasses at various times after their burial, I was astounded that the flesh disappeared, just as the soul vanished. My big question was, where did the soul go?

In fourth grade, my great grandfather Alex passed away and I attended his wake, my first funeral. Sitting in the funeral home, I was astonished to hear his soft voice tell me to smile and be happy as he lay lifeless in his casket. I checked with my sisters and they didn't hear him speak. I realized this was the first person I knew whom I could hear speak from spirit. Hearing Grandpa communicate after death was super-sensational, yet daunting at the same time!

Mentally, grandfather impressed in my mind that he was not sleeping in the casket (as my mom told me), but rather he was away visiting family members who had passed before him. He whispered reassuringly to me to be happy and help others, not to be sad when a soul returned to the world of spirit. He telepathically communicated that we would be together again and he would guide me on a life path unique to other children. Grandpa affirmed that I could hear the voice of others who had transitioned into spirit and encouraged me to attentively listen so I could share their messages with those they loved here in the physical plane. . . . Cool!

As time progressed, Grandfather helped me remember we are eternal beings of consciousness and our souls never die. He inspired me to serve spirit by accepting the honor and reverence of being a medium, a voice for beings who have crossed the bridge into spirit. What a distinctive but intimidating privilege to speak on behalf of those in spirit and demonstrate the continuity of life—the survival of consciousness beyond the death of the physical body.

SCIENTIFIC INQUIRY

With the intention to more extensively understand the human experience of spirit in a physical body, I pursued a master's in the natural sciences. My higher self and spirit guides encouraged me to learn and understand the functioning of the physical body and the sacred and incredible construction of our cellular and molecular structures. The brilliant intelligence of Source is expressed in every aspect of our body.

One afternoon, I had a momentous revelation outside the traditional classroom, when I was helping premedical students prepare a cadaver for a nursing class. While cutting into the body and identifying each astonishing organ, a thought occurred to me with uncommon clarity: This body had all the parts and systems to sustain life, but where was the unique life force switch to energize the organs so they could function like my own body? Logically and precisely, spirit had awakened my scientific mind to the existence of our life force—the spiritual aspect of our being.

As a college anatomy and physiology instructor, I learned and shared the structural genius and masterful functioning of our physical bodies. The process of natural law is expressed in the atoms, cells, tissues, and organs of the physical body. In turn, the intelligence of our physical design reveals universal understandings of the unseen aspect of ourselves.

Science is limited in fully describing the unseen and such a phenomenon as mediumship. Philosophy, while also limited, encourages rational exploration of the truths and principles of metaphysics from the experiences of being. Great philosophers such as Plato, Socrates, and Joseph Campbell, scientists such as

Carl Sagan and Albert Einstein, and psychologists such as Rudolph Steiner and Carl Jung have provided interesting perspectives of the organic universe and the limitless mind. However, the works of American mystic Edgar Cayce (1877-1945) had the greatest influence on my understanding of human consciousness and the mechanisms of mediumship. His clairvoyant channeling of insights from the unknown and knowledge of intuition as a natural process of direct knowing expanded my awareness of my higher self.

MEDIUMSHIP AND SPIRITUALITY

It wasn't by chance that my life circumstances brought me to western New York State, close to Lily Dale Assembly, the international center of modern spiritualism. For years, I studied the writings and works of famous historical mediums such as Emanuel Swedenborg, Andrew Jackson Davis, Frederic Myers, Sir Oliver Lodge, Sir Arthur Conan Doyle, Leonora Piper, and Arthur Ford. I witnessed readings by and took workshops with famous modern-day mediums such as Mavis Pittila, James Van Praagh, George Anderson, and John Edwards. All of this prepared me to share the philosophy and wisdom of the science of mediumship.

My varied work life supported my spiritual evolution. As mentioned previously, being an anatomy instructor gave me an appreciation of the human body, our vehicle for divine intelligence. Then, being a college administrator at an art school developed my clairvoyance, visual intuition, and emotional intelligence. In addition, my work as a college administrator at a university for alternative medicine helped support my understanding of the energy body and natural law.

I've explored many different religions and cultures and their unique abilities to define Truth, but I was resistant to the fear of God many religions promote. The foundation of my faith was Catholicism, and I spent hours in the church alone, reflecting. I talked to the saints and angels, who provided me with the comfort and wisdom I sought.

I've come to the conclusion I'm not a religious person—but I *am* a person of great faith. I have strong beliefs about our ability to manifest miraculous situations and Heavenly experiences as we remember our connection to the infinite, sacred, and divine Source of all that is.

Often, I'm told I am gifted for my ability to witness, consult, and comprehend my intuition and to communicate with spirits. I feel the real gift is honoring my true nature and providing the stillness within my mind to hear, feel, and see the truth of eternal existence. I now dedicate my life to the science of mediumship, the universal laws of nature, the exploration of infinite consciousness, and a better acquaintance with the I AM Presence.

I briefly share my story so you might understand my unique scientific, philosophical, and intuitive perspective. I blend the intellectual, religious, and rational with my intrinsic intuition to provide you with a simple understanding of mediumship and help you experience its natural process.

CONSCIOUSNESS AND ENLIGHTENMENT

My life as a student is continuous. I read, meditate, and study as well as lecture, discuss, and write about the boundless abilities of our consciousness.

Humanity continues to explore the limitless possibilities of the universe. As we learn about the expansiveness of our collective consciousness and the astounding reality of our spirit, we can experience the wonderment of truth and our virtuous existence. Many wise teachers have remembered this truth, such as Jesus, Buddha, the Dalai Lama, and Chief White Eagle, to name only a few.

The histories of numerous cultures and societies include stories of communicating with spirits through saints, sages, shamans, and others. We celebrate these messages as the word of God, the voice of angels, the expression of universal consciousness, the wisdom of ancestors, and the like.

I share ideas and experiences with you that have helped me understand the universal nature of divine intelligence. That said, the process of enlightenment does not require completing studies, classes, workshops, or ceremonies, or achieving a title or degree. Enlightenment is simply removing the obstacles you have accepted and built up against the nature of your sacred and true self. It is remembering and experiencing your heavenly essence as a divine being of light.

I share my story of enlightenment only as an example of one of millions of souls who experience the universe with a conscious and disciplined awareness. It's my hope that you can become more familiar with the art, science, and philosophy of mediumship. Connecting with your loved ones in the spiritual plane can't help but expand your own consciousness.

THE WORLD OF SPIRIT AND SPIRIT COMMUNICATION

That life is eternal
And love is immortal
And death is only a horizon
Life is eternal
As we move into the light
And a horizon is nothing
Save the limit of our sight.

"Life is Eternal" ~ Carly Simon

Within the body's shell, your spirit has a limited perspective when exploring the realms of reality using only your physical senses. However, scientific instruments can demonstrate the existence of things beyond the scope of the average human's physical ability to witness and understand. For example, the fields of vibrational and energy medicine employ technologies to measure the human energy field, and the aura can now be captured with Kirlian photography.

As you elevate your consciousness during meditation, contemplation, dreaming, and doing activities that bring forth your passion, you can sense other realms outside the limitations of your physical world. As Carly Simon so wisely sings, "death is only a horizon." Beyond that horizon is a new dimension of existence you can't see until you get there. The life of your spirit is eternal, and the scope and perspective of your spiritual nature is much more comprehensive and expansive than you can imagine.

Many times, clients receiving a reading inquire as to where their loved ones went when they left their physical body. The world of spirit that's home to these loved ones exists in a plane of higher vibration than this physical plane. Just as multiple frequencies of radio waves exist in the same space, the physical and spiritual planes overlap. You normally can't see your loved ones in spirit because they're vibrating at a higher frequency than you are. However, they have the ability to feel your presence and hear your inner voice. They know when you feel sad or happy, when you feel love or fear, guilt or innocence.

Often during a reading, those in spirit will encourage those receiving the message to accept their own loving, kind, and compassionate nature and surrender their grief, shame, or guilt. They constantly remind my clients that their love is eternal and it's best to focus their attention on those they're currently sharing their life with on the physical plane.

From the perspective of your loved ones in the spiritual realm, they don't miss you because they don't have the illusionary limitations you have in the physical world. They understand you will always be together and nothing except the mistaken belief within your ego-mind can prevent them from communicating with you on a continuous basis. All you have to do is feel them in your heart and accept that your love is everlasting.

Often, I'm asked what the world of spirit is like. I believe the book called *What Dreams May Come* by Richard Matheson demonstrates that the afterlife is determined by your soul's own belief system. Your imagination creates the experience. If you believe the world of spirit is a garden, a forest, a mountain, a cloud, or a reality similar to our natural world, you will manifest that reality.

Validations from evidential mediumship prove that your loved ones exist beyond the death of their physical body. For more than one hundred years, professional mediums have maintained the existence of the world of spirit and have provided messages from those who have passed over of how much freedom, independence, and serenity they experience in spirit.

Two of the great pioneers of the modern Spiritualism movement, Emanuel Swedenborg and Andrew Jackson Davis, refer to the world of spirit as Summerland, a place of great beauty and peace. Based on their spirit communications, these spiritualists believed Summerland to be a place of rest for souls in between their incarnations on the earth plane, where souls reflect on their life and the lessons they learned. In the splendor and tranquility of Summerland, souls have happy reunions with deceased family members and friends and share their memories.

Your loved ones in spirit are not far from your thoughts. Just imagine them on a relaxing and healing vacation enjoying the magnificence of a heavenly place of sharing, inspiration, and enlightenment. Call them to you and send your love, affection, and kindness. They are eager to give you uplifting messages and let you in on truths that are obscured by the realities of the earth plane.

SPIRIT COMMUNICATION

The main purpose of spirit communication is to support the natural law that life is continuous and eternal! Therefore, consciousness survives the death of the physical body. Beyond that, spirits have many reasons to give messages, such as those of encouragement, direction, appreciation, and wisdom. As a sitter, you may also seek knowledge about your karma, soul agreements, and the emotional and mental obstacles preventing you from knowing peace and joy.

When you receive a reading, your loved ones in spirit present themselves according to several variables. These usually include: the most pressing issues in your life, the amount of comfort the spirit has with the medium, your own level of awareness, and most important, your intentions for the reading. Certain spirits may present messages relating to particular issues and circumstances in your life. For example, each spirit may choose to provide messages in a certain area or areas, such as career, parenting, family conflicts, romance, karma, life path, health issues, and many more.

Just as you have free will to have a reading, your loved ones in spirit have the freedom to choose whether or not they will communicate during the reading. It's rare that specific loved ones don't show up for a reading. They are usually most eager to share messages to support and encourage your spiritual growth and your earthly well-being. The sequence in which spirits present themselves during a reading is astonishing to me. They know when they have information that will be most helpful for you at any given time.

The magic, or mysticism, of a reading is how your loved ones inspire the mind of the medium to present original messages you will recognize or can verify after the reading. As the saying goes, a picture is worth a thousand words. For the medium, the process involves opening the mind to act like a blank movie screen to allow spirits to send images, feelings, and sounds that both the medium and sitter can relate to and understand. A message can have many layers, with both literal and symbolic significance. It's up to you, the sitter, to fully and personally interpret the message.

It's vital for the spirit, the medium, and the sitter (you) to all actively work to support the enchanted process of mediumship. The more engaged you are with the process, the more insightful wisdom and compassionate understanding you will obtain from the reading. Be open, honest, and willing to research the things that don't make sense to you at the time of the reading. I feel it's most important for you to record the reading and/or take notes during the reading so you can refer to the messages later and perhaps gain a higher awareness from them.

A medium isn't always necessary because your loved ones are constantly communicating with genuine signs and messages of encouragement. However, a medium may be able to bring in more specific messages and provide more clarity and understanding or a different perspective. It would be my pleasure to serve as the intermediary between you and your loved ones in spirit, to help share their communications so you can feel their presence and know their love.

PURPOSE AND PROCESS

The purpose of this book is threefold. Besides commemorating my twenty-five inspiring years as a professional intuitive medium, I want to show my appreciation to the spirit world. In addition, I'd like to share what I've learned and give others a better understanding of this spiritual realm and my communication process.

As an intuitive medium, I've learned to more clearly understand, firsthand from higher levels of consciousness, the purpose and meaning of life and the laws of nature. It's been my great pleasure to be reminded that consciousness survives the death of the physical body because our souls are eternal and divine. To sense the presence of a spirit I can't see with my physical eyes, hear with my ears, or touch with my hands is nothing short of astonishing. To be able to communicate with loved ones from the spirit world is one of my greatest achievements; to share their healing and inspiring messages of gratitude, encouragement, loving kindness, and forgiveness is one of my greatest joys.

The magnificence of mediumship is reflected in the brilliant wisdom, expansive understanding, and affectionate feeling of thoughtfulness it offers those open to receive it. My responsibility as an intuitive medium is to blend my higher consciousness with the consciousness of loved ones in spirit and deliver their messages with precision, purpose, and reason.

FOUR MAIN ASPECTS

The process of mediumship intermingles four main aspects: the medium, the sitter (the person receiving the reading), the spirits, and the messages. The following parts of this book address each area in turn to help you better appreciate the mechanics of a reading and my philosophy of mediumship. I hope this approach will also help you get the most out of a reading, should you choose to experience one.

Optimal spirit communication occurs when the spirit, the sitter, and the medium are focused, present, and completely open. This synergy increases the likelihood that the message will be strong, clearly received, and well understood.

In each of the following parts, I share stories of readings that gifted the sitters and me with precious messages of kindheartedness and inspired wisdom. These clients have given me permission to provide evidence and insights from the messages they received. I've altered their names and intermixed readings to protect each sitter's identity and emphasize specific ideas and comparable thoughts. My intention is to clarify the purpose of mediumship, and most important, the various types of messages received. I have not exaggerated or changed the messages as I remember them to the best of my ability. I wish to sincerely share with you the bewildering process of mediumship and how truly healing messages from the world of spirit can be.

Writing *Lasting Impressions* strengthened my gratefulness for the miraculous messages received from spirit over the years. As I reflected on my experiences as an intuitive medium, I realized how spiritually mystical and divine each soul is, and that souls maintain an everlasting connection.

To clarify, I may use the term *spirit* by itself to represent the world of spirit or spirits in the aggregate, whereas the term *spirits* refers to more than one spirit or specific spirits. The term *soul* or *souls* is often used interchangeably with *spirit* or *spirits,* as in the above paragraph, but beyond that, there's a fine distinction. A spirit, or individual in the spiritual plane, *has* a soul, which is that person or spirit's divine, eternal essence, or Higher Self. A spirit can experience growth and transformation, whereas a soul needs no transformation and is always the essence of love and perfection.

I hope this book, and these stories, help you more fully recognize that you are eternal—and your love is forever.

PART 2
THE MEDIUM

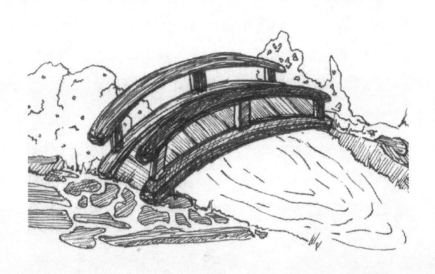

THE MEDIUM ~ THE BRIDGE

When you're weary, feeling small,
When tears are in your eyes
I will dry them all
I'm on your side
When times get rough
And friends just can't be found
Like a bridge over troubled water
I will lay me down

"Bridge Over Troubled Water"
~ Simon and Garfunkel

As a medium, it's my privilege to be a bridge between the physical and spiritual worlds to share wisdom, affection, and encouragement from the higher perspective of souls in the spiritual plane to ease the sitter's mind. I'm not unique in my ability to communicate with spirit; we all have the ability to see, hear, and mostly feel, the presence of spirit. My gift is in my ability to mentally focus and trust what I receive.

When I offer a reading, I'm often reminded by my clients' loved ones in spirit that I'm speaking on their behalf and therefore they must trust my intentions. They appreciate my efforts. It seems as though they choose a medium—or rather encourage the sitter to choose a specific medium—to allow their messages to come through with clarity and truth. Therefore, a sitter's reading begins far in advance of the actual meeting time with the medium.

ETERNAL LIFE AND LOVE

To reiterate, the foundation of mediumship is the universal law that life is eternal and that the existence and personal identity of a soul continues after the change called death. Death only occurs to the physical body, but the soul remains alive forever; it cannot be created or destroyed. Mediumship also reminds us of the universal law of love—that love is also eternal. Love is all that truly exists. Our task is to remove all barriers we have built up against the idea that we are love and everyone is love. Love is our purpose for being!

A medium is an intermediary, bringing specific messages from the higher vibrations of the spiritual plane to the lower vibrations of the physical plane. Your loved ones in the spirit plane provide specific clues, or evidence, to help you identify them and then provide inspirational messages to encourage and support you and/or clarify your life purpose. It's such a pleasure to be the messenger from one loving soul to another.

Note that for you to carry your own messages to your loved ones in spirit, a medium is not necessary. Your loved ones in the spiritual plane hear and feel you whenever you call their name.

MENTAL AND PHYSICAL MEDIUMSHIP

There are two major types of mediumship: mental and physical. Mental mediumship involves the telepathic communication from the consciousness of the spirit to the medium. Physical mediumship is the manipulation and transformation of energy to cause a sound, movement, or result that's perceived by your physical senses. For example, the voice of the incarnate spirit might come through, or the spirit might move your keys, flicker your lights, or present the aroma of a scent associated with them.

24

Forms of Mental Mediumship

I practice mental mediumship, which involves three main forms of communication. My strongest form of mental mediumship is clairaudience, or clear hearing. I can hear spirits speak from their high vibration, and therefore, it's easy for me to do phone readings and hear specific messages. With mental concentration, I can hear spirits speak with my "intuitive ears." In certain circumstances, I can hear accents, sounds associated with their hobbies or career, or songs they liked. To not only hear the sounds but also know the meaning and feeling associated with the sounds is important in conveying the messages.

A second form of mental mediumship is called clairvoyance, or clear seeing. In visions, I can see images, symbols, or signs and know their specific meanings. Your loved ones in spirit like to choose special associations they shared with you or had a passion for themselves. A grandma who liked to bake may present pies, cookies, or cakes; a grandpa who liked to build things may present his tools. A child who enjoyed music may present musical instruments; a mom who was a banker may show money and checks. This visual evidence I receive helps you to identify them.

The third form of mental mediumship is clairsentience, or clear feeling. I may experience sensations within my solar plexus or heart center (gut feelings) or sensations on the surface of my body (mostly my arms and shoulders). With clairsentience, I can also obtain information through my sense of smell and taste. During a reading, your loved one might provide the scent of roses if that person had a passion for gardening, or the smell of fresh-cut grass if the person enjoyed time in the yard. Creatively, your loved one in spirit might manifest within my mouth the taste of a specific food that person enjoyed or present a feeling of a fear or joy the person carried when in the earth plane. Often, I can feel bodily sensations where the individual had been affected by the discomforts of disease or injury.

Signs and Symbols

My scientific mind often takes me to the logistics and deeper meanings of the messages presented by spirit. Of great value, though, is for you to validate with your feelings the evidence and inspirational messages presented to you. If something doesn't feel right to you, you needn't accept it. Take time to reflect on your messages and feel the associations with them to your loved ones. One of the great benefits of a reading is that your loved ones in spirit will validate what you already feel and help you develop a means of communication with them using specific signs. For example, they might show me a butterfly, a pizza, a kite, irises, or coins; they might sing "Somewhere Over the Rainbow" or say a specific term of endearment. Feel your messages because spirit communication is all about feeling your loved one.

HELP AND PREPARATION

As a medium, I do have my limitations. Some spirits, just like people, are challenging to communicate with. If I can't understand a specific spirit, I ask for the assistance of another loved one of the sitter or my own loved ones in spirit. At times, I may have many spirits working with me to provide the most successful message so the sitter has the ultimate opportunity to learn or be encouraged. Imagine when you are trying to communicate with more than one person at a time. It takes a lot of concentration!

Preparing for a spiritual reading, I sit in silence and align with my highly sensitive nature as a psychic and intuitive. Initially, I feel the energetic aura of sitters to sense their feelings, concerns, challenges, and beliefs about their karma, as well as what healing their soul is pursuing. After assessing the aura of the sitter, I welcome in those loved ones from the spirit world who can best encourage, support, inspire, and help that person.

Mediumship takes years of development and practice, no matter what someone's innate abilities may be. As with anything, the more practice and experience someone has with a specific skill, the greater knowledge, wisdom, and understanding the person develops over time.

Over the years, I have established a personal code for communicating with spirits based on my specific background and life experiences. My strong connection with nature allows spirit to be more sensitive to the lessons and wisdom of nature, and often spirit uses symbols from nature to share a message. For example, as a biologist and avid hiker, spirit can present a hiking trail to help me understand an emotional or mental challenge a sitter may be experiencing or a type of tree to represent the sitter's physical strength. Since communication is mostly feeling based, spirit knows and understands to use symbols I can fully feel and sense.

The universe rejoices with its wisdom and often awakens us to its insight using serendipity and synchronicity. All timing is divine, in universal terms. Continually, I am gifted by spirit presenting complementary messages within a short period of time to reinforce the splendor of their passion to work with us here on the earth plane. For example, I will have a series of readings about moms with memory problems before they passed, dads with a specific hobby or occupation, sons who passed from drug overdoses, or daughters who took their own life all clustered within a short period of time. Perhaps the synchronicity in messages is due to spirits working together to better serve their loved ones and make it easier for the medium. No matter (literally); it's amazing how connected everything is and how messages from spirit attract similar spirits with like messages.

Allow me to present several readings that emphasize my role as a medium—an intermediary bridge between two parallel planes of existence. The intense concentration of listening, seeing, and feeling is important in providing messages of clarity and purpose.

MERRY CHRISTMAS, FROM DAD

Pulling up to the airport departure doors, from the security of my parents' minivan, my heart hammered with uneasiness. Once again, it was time for me to clumsily say that awkward goodbye to my family. Focusing my attention on getting my boarding passes and enduring the long ATF security-check line distracted me somewhat from my sadness.

Once I got through security, I sat at my gate to reflect for a few moments on the wonderful and tasty holiday memories I'd just enjoyed with my family. Then I opened myself up to serve Spirit in whatever way possible. Making my airport connections to safely return to Palm Springs was minor compared to the spiritual mission soon to come my way.

Once I was seated on the plane, a tall gentleman in his twenties with an anxious gaze sat next to me. I sensed a strong feeling of apprehension as his hand tightly clasped a book about running and meditation, two of my favorite hobbies.

Immediately we connected on the subject of running, hiking, and our unique scientific career paths. Even though Kyle was an educated computer software specialist, his mind was open to expand beyond the idea of the physical world. I explained how I'd been home visiting family and traveling to teach workshops on seeing and sensing auras. He was intrigued and asked many questions about the human energy field and the soul.

Taking a chance, I asked him why he harbored guilt, shame, and a sense of regret in his aura. Luckily, he wasn't offended. Kyle explained that his father had passed a few years back and he had promised his dad that he would always go home for Christmas, his mom's favorite holiday. He felt a strong sense of sadness saying goodbye to his mom and guilt at leaving her.

I then asked him if it would be all right if I connected with the consciousness of his father. He had no idea I was a medium, but I felt his father was determined to find a way to communicate with his son.

I said that I sensed the name James and he was playing an organ. I heard sacred church music like Handel's *Messiah* and Sunday favorites like "How Great Thou Art." I also saw this man changing notes with his pencil on lined paper. Kyle's face lit up with a healing grin as his eyes filled with tears of joy. He confirmed that his father James had been the choir director at his church and had played the organ. Kyle also confirmed other information I received about his father. He had endured a long illness associated with his lungs and throat, he loved to read historical novels, and he frequently traveled to national parks to appreciate the beauty of nature. Kyle said his best memories with his father were their annual trips to hike and camp in the national parks of the western United States.

The healing message James gifted to his son was not to feel distress about leaving his mom, although he appreciated Kyle's visit home to share the special holiday. He wanted Kyle to know he should continue his dream of being a musician and composing music with his guitar. Although they both chose different musical instruments to work with and very different music styles, James inspired and encouraged his son to follow his passion. Kyle wept with a sense of relief in releasing the guilt he had for leaving his mom and felt a renewed sense of optimism about his desire to compose music.

James asked Kyle to tell his mom he loved her holiday ham and potatoes au gratin. He was glad the family still attended midnight mass together and maintained the family tradition of singing Christmas carols after dinner. He reminded Kyle that music provided the ideal energy to enhance the special moments of life.

With my clairsentience, I smelled hot cocoa, and Kyle shared that each Christmas Eve, after everyone else went to bed, he had enjoyed a cup of cocoa with his dad.

People in our row and the row behind us were listening to the reading and everyone had tears in their eyes as they felt the tremendous healing these messages brought to this young man. The flight attendant came to our row to ask if everything was all right and we all nodded yes with smiles.

Kyle let me know he was stuck in a job that he had no passion for and wanted to return to composing music and playing his guitar in a band. He was living in Nevada and had moved there with three hometown friends as they had a rock band. His three buddies had given up their dream of music to raise families, and Kyle had gotten a job at a software company. His father encouraged him to teach music lessons, reconnect with the music contacts he had, and dedicate time each week to composing his music.

Next, I heard another fatherly voice come through from spirit, and I received impressions of a gentleman who had suffered paralysis from a disease. He provided the name Polly. Kyle was dazed by this message from Lenny, his girlfriend Polly's father, in spirit, whom he'd never met. Lenny communicated to Kyle to let his daughter know he is proud of her work as an administrator with community service programs and that he supports her decision to leave law school. Lenny conveyed his passion for birds of prey and asked Kyle to share with Polly that when she sees an owl, her father is sending a compassionate sign of his presence. He also showed me all types of colorful lilies, and I could smell their sweetness in a large backyard garden with a winding cobblestone path.

Kyle was so overwhelmed with his reading he sat for two hours in silence with his mind processing the messages. As soon as we landed, he phoned his girlfriend and I heard, "You won't believe what just happened on my flight. . . ." Polly confirmed that her father loved owls and his greatest passion had been his garden, which her mother still maintained in the backyard. When Polly was just twelve, she helped her parents place the stones for the path. Shortly after that, she told Kyle, her dad developed Parkinson's disease and passed within a few years.

Because I had passions similar to those of both these fathers, I could relate to the signs and messages they wanted to convey to their children. That's why they chose me to help them bring encouragement and loving support.

I thanked Spirit for allowing me to be the messenger and departed the plane. Kyle caught up to me in the airport, shook my hand, and thanked me for the greatest Christmas present of all. Then he told me what Polly had said on the phone. Ironically, his girlfriend Polly had been researching mediums to find one to give him a reading for his Christmas present.

Kyle's hopeful stride and enthusiastic smile brought joy to my heart, knowing his perception of his life had been uplifted and his passion for music was very much alive. Joy to the world!

MUSIC TO MY EARS

When I lived in my Long Beach condo, I often sat outside the secured building to meet clients, awaiting their arrival. One cold, rainy, and windy day, I sat in the ballroom waiting for my next client, protected from the weather. I couldn't help but look at the lonely and aged grand piano, sitting in the corner of the shady room. Mentally, I could hear a familiar 70s song, as if the piano were playing itself. Then I heard the famous singer adding his lyrics to the piano melody. Like a broken record, over and over I kept hearing these lyrics (I would share the song, but I must maintain the privacy of my client). In my mind, instead of this poor old grand piano, I saw the singer at a shiny white grand piano, and he had a microphone and some type of music statues on his piano. A distinct, deep baritone voice sang loudly through my mind along with the impeccable piano playing until the sitter showed up at my door.

I could tell this spirit was very excited to visit with his loved one. He understood my passion for music and that I had studied music for many years—especially voice and some piano. I felt he genuinely thought I would be helpful to relate musical metaphors to his daughter coming for the reading.

Carol was very nervous, and she insisted on giving me only her first name for fear I might google information about her. A young lady in her early thirties, she was beautifully dressed, with a gorgeous turquoise aura around her. Although I didn't recognize her, I immediately felt she was a singer who hadn't been performing for some time. She acknowledged that she loved to sing and had sung for years, but since her father's passing, she had lost the desire to sing.

As is my practice, I inquired why she came for a reading. Carol explained that she'd lost a few very significant people in her life and wanted to communicate with them. Her voice began to shake when she told me she'd had no time for goodbyes with these loved ones.

Initially, I felt the presence of a grandmother on her father's side, and I could hear the grandma mentally say, "She is my namesake." Carol confirmed that she was named for her Grandma Carol, but I heard a "Gi" sound. Grandma Carol impressed in my mind that she had been a gospel singer and had sung in church in front of large audiences. She loved to wear the color purple, lots of gold jewelry, and always a big floppy hat. I saw beautiful snow white lilies and Carol confirmed that lilies were Grandma's favorite flower. She also said the other information communicated was correct about Grandma: She was a well known gospel singer and especially liked wearing purple and a big hat. Carol added that they often called her Gigi.

With my clairaudience, I could hear "We Shall Overcome" and felt Gigi loved to sing this song. Carol verified that this song was her grandma's favorite and she was often asked to sing it in church. In fact, Gigi sang this song to Carol often when Carol was brushing her teeth for bed.

Carol asked if Grandma Gigi felt better. I was encouraged to communicate that Gigi had a painful experience with colon cancer and had also lost her legs to diabetes. As Gigi had done in the physical, she answered her granddaughter with the lyrics to "Oh, Happy Day," and Carol smiled through tears. Gigi asked Carol to follow her passion to sing and share her healing voice in dedication to God and all people.

I felt that Gigi had heaviness in her chest before she passed and couldn't breathe. Carol confirmed that Gigi had passed from pneumonia and she was unable to see her before she passed away. Carol began to cry, and Gigi communicated it was best she didn't see her at the end when she was ill. She asked Carol not to worry about not being there; Carol had often visited her when she was well.

The main reason Carol came to the reading was to hear from Gigi but also someone else highly important to her. Gigi said she wanted to present her son, Carol's father, the spirit who had visited with me before Carol arrived. I felt the presence of a very large man sitting at a white grand piano, singing his heart away. The song I heard him sing was the one playing through my mind before Carol arrived. Also, I saw handwritten sheets of music, which I felt implied he composed his own music. With more tears, Carol nodded to confirm this information. Her father showed me newspapers and magazines with the initials of his name, and then I saw a star plaque on Hollywood Boulevard with his initials on it. Carol confirmed her father was a composer and famous singer. How cool, I thought, to be connecting with a musical genius.

Charles had a distinctive voice, and I could feel his words intensely as he wanted to let his daughter know how much he loved her. He asked for her forgiveness for leaving her before she entered high school but assured her he had great memories of her. He showed me a large stuffed lion. Carol smiled and said that was her favorite toy from her dad. Charles wanted her to know the lion represented courage and inner strength, and he would always send her that.

Just as her grandma had done, Charles encouraged Carol to sing again. He urged her to take voice lessons and create music because he knew this was her passion. He told her to go into her bedroom closet and get out her old journals and continue to write—that he would be her muse. Carol couldn't believe her father knew about her music journals in her closet, and she was overwhelmed that he wanted her to write and perform. She couldn't remember where she'd put her journals but said she'd look for them when she returned home to Los Angeles.

Before leaving my mind, Charles said his favorite photo of Carol was of the two of them sitting at the piano playing, and she was in a white dress. With amusement, Carol acknowledged she kept that photo on her nightstand and it was her great memory, too. In fact, Carol had her father's piano bench from that very photo, which was all she had of his belongings.

Carol asked why her father left so quickly. He conveyed that his heart could no longer function and that he was greatly sad for the lack of respect from those he loved in his life in his later years. He communicated that he'd been quite selfish and his ego-mind had wanted more and more attention. Wisely, he wanted Carol to know that passion for his music was the only thing that mattered because he knew it helped people heal through troubled relationships, like his own.

He urged Carol to not allow the music industry to decide what music to write. Carol explained to me that for many years she'd written lyrics and hidden them away. Her father encouraged her to get back to creating music as it would awaken her heart and soul. He reminded her she already had enough music to make an album. He said to write from the passion within her heart and soul. Carol looked stunned, but I sensed a renewed sense of hope for her creating and performing her music.

Carol asked who her daddy was with in Heaven (the spiritual plane). I was surprised to learn that many singers from the 40s through the 80s were all together. I could hear and sense specific songs, including those of Elvis Presley, Dionne Warwick, Michael Jackson, and Sammy Davis Jr., just to name a few. He also communicated to his daughter that he'd found Jack in spirit and he was pleased to share his appreciation for all that Jack had done to help him with his career. Carol established that Jack had been her dad's manager, who had influenced his music career for over forty years.

In closing, I asked Carol how she found me as a medium. She explained that in the last few months she had missed her father so much that she'd asked many friends to recommend a spiritual reader they trusted. Although her friends offered her names, none of them resonated with her. When she listened to her father's music, she kept seeing the letter "G" and felt this referred to a local medium. She researched mediums, and when she saw my name, she felt her father had selected me.

FINDING JOY

Sue, a close family friend, asked for a reading to connect with her mother Joy, who had passed from many years of medical problems and Alzheimer's. When I'm asked to do a reading for someone I know to connect with someone I knew who passed, I want to ensure I'm as impartial as possible presenting evidence and inspiring messages.

As a former scientist and an analytical guy, it's important to me when connecting with a spirit that I provide the sitter with at least several unique but simple pieces of evidence about the person in spirit. I want to know—and the sitter to know with assurance—with whom I am communicating.

Joy had been a scientist herself, and her spirit was confident I could convey her love and gratitude to her daughter.

I'd been acquainted with Sue's mom Joy for many years but had only seen her once in the last five years of her life. From my limited knowledge, I knew that Joy enjoyed tennis, golf, and shopping, so I asked Joy's spirit, in my mind, to share something unfamiliar to me but that Sue would know. Joy communicated that Sue had brought homemade meals to her in the nursing home where she'd lived almost every day for over five years, even though full-service meals were provided. The fish, mashed potatoes, and peach pie were some of Joy's favorites, she conveyed to me. This hit home in Sue's heart. She validated that she'd brought her mom meals and her mom loved her broiled fish and homemade fruit pies.

With my intuitive ears, I heard Joy say she loved playing

41

bridge—and gambling at casinos in Niagara Falls and Las Vegas with Sue. She communicated that she knew Sue had recently won several thousand dollars on the penny slots as a way to let Sue know she was with her. She also communicated she was pleased that Sue's son Curt had decided to move back to the East Coast from LA and assured her he would have a much more comfortable and fulfilling lifestyle.

Sue was crying as she confirmed that just last month she'd won almost $3,000 on the slots and that she often thought of her mom when she was at the casino. Curt had moved to Virginia the previous week, Sue explained, and she was so happy her mom was watching over him.

In my mind, I could hear "The Wedding March" and saw a bride with a golden heart-shaped pendant around her neck. Joy conveyed that she had been at this wedding and she would always be a guardian to the bride. Sue told me that her granddaughter Lisa had been married several months before, and on her wedding day, Sue had given her Joy's heart-shaped pendant to let her know her great grandma was with her. Sue kept saying, "I can't believe it. I really just can't believe it."

Sue kept a spotless house, and her mom had often joked with her about it. She referred to the hours Sue spent in the laundry room, acknowledging that she still loved to sit with her while Sue folded and ironed the clothes. Sue told me she had washed her mom's bed sheets weekly and would bring them to the nursing home. Her mom was so appreciative to Sue for all the loving care she'd given her, especially in the last years of her life.

Sue was comforted when her mom communicated that she was with both her older sisters, who had passed before her. Clairvoyantly, I saw all three sisters laughing on a cruise ship in a tropical environment with lots of islands. Sue shared that the ladies had taken several trips to the Caribbean when they were all healthy. Both of Joy's sisters thanked Sue for all she had done to care for her mom and let her know they would be helping her adjust to the spiritual plane. They reminded Sue to have a hot fudge sundae to celebrate her kindness and sweetness. Sue laughed because her aunts had often taken her for sundaes, her favorite dessert.

Sue's aunts presented the image of three little songbirds singing. With a smile, Sue said that many mornings she noticed three finches from her kitchen window on her clothesline. This sign that her mom was with her sisters consoled her.

A white-haired man appeared in my mind, and he communicated he passed from lung cancer and had loved to golf with Joy. He showed me piles of money and ledger sheets. He had a ring on with the initial "I." Sue confirmed that Ivan was her mom's late husband and that he'd been a banker who passed from lung cancer. She was pleased her mom had found him in the spirit plane and that he visited for the reading. Mainly, Ivan wanted to communicate to Sue that her mom was well connected to family members in spirit, and he thanked her for accepting him into their family late in life.

It had been eighteen months since Sue's mom had passed and she missed her so much. Toward the end of the reading, Sue asked how she could be sure her mom was with her. Spirit often reminds me that the strongest sign is feeling our loved ones' presence; our hearts are eternally connected. But skeptical, Sue asked for a specific sign. I saw laundry hanging on the clothesline and a colorful group of tulips blossoming in my mind. This got Sue's attention because she had received a large pot of tulips from her friends when her mom passed and had buried the bulbs outside her kitchen window. She told me, though, that she was disappointed the tulips hadn't blossomed the previous spring. Sue thanked me for the messages and said she would watch for the presence of her mother.

To close the reading, Joy conveyed to Sue that she is always with her and hears her prayers.

Several months later, Sue phoned me with excitement. The tulips blossomed with snow still on the ground, in early March, even before the crocuses budded. Sue was thrilled because the flowers blossomed the week of her mom's birthday. Joy communicated that the perpetual blossoming of the tulips was symbolic of how the soul thrives with inner beauty and never dies.

Two months later, Sue was doing laundry on Mother's Day and was feeling the emptiness of no longer having a mom to celebrate with. As she removed fresh sheets from the dryer, she noticed that a white tag was caught in the lint trap. Startled and delighted, Sue saw the name Joy in her handwriting.

Several years before, when Joy had gone into the nursing home, Sue had labeled all her clothing with tags, and she remembered from her reading that her mom said she would be with her while she was doing her household chores. Immediately, Sue phoned me and explained she'd found "Joy" that day!

BILL'S BILL

Before the radiant glow of the new day, I entered the pandemonium of the airport to catch my flight for a series of lectures and workshops in the Midwest. Arriving early, I decided to go on standby for an earlier flight, thinking I would have more time to grab breakfast with a longer layover. I missed getting on the flight by just one person but accepted that I was supposed to be on my original flight for some reason. I couldn't help but notice a lady who walked into the gate area wearing a vibrant pink jumpsuit with matching hat and shoes. Intuitively, I knew I would be sitting next to her on the plane, and that pink would be my morning coffee. I felt the presence of a spirit who wanted to share an important message with her.

Sure enough, Kathy, the lady in pink, was divinely seated next to me, and she kindly introduced herself before she even sat down. Her personality was as golden as her hair, and her deep laugh was therapeutic. As the sun began to peek up over the mountains, with a hint of hope, the plane taxied down the runway. Before our plane left the ground, she asked me if I knew of a good medium her daughter and she could go to. Again, I smiled, recognizing the awesome element of divine timing and intervention by the Universe. I was sitting next to just the right person.

Instantly, I felt the presence of a male spirit, professionally dressed with bright new running shoes, and I felt he had had problems with his heart. He showed me he was wearing white, which meant he was associated with the medical field. I saw him in a home office, and

47

he communicated his wife had worked with him. Kathy confirmed that her husband had recently passed from a heart attack, he'd been a doctor with his own practice, she'd been the office manager for the practice, and his passion had been running long distances.

He showed me mid-February on a calendar, near Valentine's Day, as being special, and Kathy confirmed their anniversary was in mid-February. He then communicated to me thirty-nine years. Bill had passed away of heart failure the day before their fortieth wedding anniversary, Kathy explained. I saw him smiling, and through me, he told her to feel no guilt for not being present when he passed on.

Kathy whispered she had been in Palm Springs visiting with her parents on their seventieth wedding anniversary, and that her own fortieth anniversary was on the exact same day. Her husband Bill had surprised her by gifting her with a trip to the desert so she could spend the special day with her parents. When she returned, they were to celebrate their own anniversary.

On the day of Kathy's parents' seventieth anniversary, her father had a heart attack and flatlined. After several minutes, her ninety-two-year-old father just woke up as if he'd simply been napping. Kathy had called an ambulance and traveled with her parents to the hospital. While driving to the hospital, Kathy received a phone call from her son and he sadly informed her that Bill had passed away on the couch. Kathy learned that her father and husband had had heart attacks within minutes of each other. Bill decided to leave for the spirit plane just as her father returned to the earth plane.

In my mind, I saw a backyard in-ground swimming pool and an elaborate brick grilling pit. Bill conveyed that some of his fondest memories were being with the boys and their families each summer. He asked Kathy to tell the boys he loved them and he appreciated their efforts as coaches to their kids and supportive sons to their mom. With a warm smile, Kathy acknowledged they had two sons, Justin and Joel, who each had a son they coached on their respective baseball teams. Her eyes began to water as she told me how Bill made each summer so special with his family and how he loved to barbecue on their sophisticated grill he'd built himself.

Bill encouraged me to share a message about a check she'd received as a sign that he was present, and I could hear the Frank Sinatra song "My Way." Kathy's eyes brightened with the luminescence of hope as she explained that Frank was his favorite singer. As she pondered the message from the other side, she recalled that on the day she received a bill in her mailbox for $3,640 for his cremation, she'd also received a long overdue check from one of Bill's patients. The check was for the exact same amount of $3,640. Bill's bill was covered by a paid debt from many years ago, and Bill wanted Kathy to know she would be provided for. Love has no boundaries, and our connections are everlasting, from lifetime to lifetime.

Inquisitively, Kathy asked if I felt Bill was her soul mate. As spirit has impressed upon me, a soul mate is any soul who has helped you to shift your beliefs or has inspired your mind, encouraged your self-love, and/or enlightened your soul with sacred wisdom. Soul mates can come in antagonistic forms, causing conflict, or as wise, compassionate teachers. I told Kathy I felt she and Bill had had at least several past lives together, and she curiously asked if I could connect with one.

Using my insightful intuition, I explained to Kathy that I could try to take a look at her Akashic Records, or the records of her soul. She looked puzzled so I explained that a record of every lifetime a soul has experienced is maintained within a sacred library of the soul. Through higher consciousness, some people are able to connect to the Akashic Records and glimpse past lives with the intention of greater understanding of soul agreements or how to heal.

By concentrating for a few moments, in my mind I saw Kathy as a poor servant girl, working in the kitchen of an extensive country estate outside of Edinburgh, Scotland, in the 1600s. I saw that her family lived in servant quarters on the estate and that Bill was the eldest son of the lord of the estate. Bill had a highly privileged life, with private tutors. His family prepared him to take over the family business, but his passion was to study medicine. His father supported only his education associated with the family business. Reluctantly, Bill accepted and effectively expanded the family business. He fell in love with Kathy, which was forbidden, and they kept their affair secret. When Bill's father found out about his secret affair, he politically arranged for Bill to marry into another wealthy family to merge their businesses. Bill reluctantly accepted his father's offer and lived a wealthy life in a loveless marriage.

The story seemed sad to Kathy, but she was amazed because she and Bill had visited Scotland and it felt like home to them. They had had plans to return there before he suddenly passed. She also explained that, in this lifetime, Bill had been in a previous marriage his family had encouraged, and he had met Kathy when she came to work in his doctor's office. She smiled, realizing that this time around he not only got to be a doctor but eventually married her.

Bill wanted to tell us both that he helped us to connect on this flight so he could surprise her with messages. Our connections to anatomy and running gave Bill the confidence to use my skills as a medium to share his messages.

In closing, Bill communicated how beautiful his funeral had been and how pleased he felt that his boys had spoken at the service. In my mind, he showed me a rainbow and I could hear bagpipes playing. Kathy grabbed my hand tightly and her tears kept flowing. She was speechless for a moment. Then she explained that on the day of Bill's funeral, it had poured rain all day, but when they arrived at the cemetery, the rain suddenly stopped. The sun peeked out from behind the clouds, and as she was leaving the cemetery, Kathy saw a rainbow. With enthusiasm, she said, "I knew it was from my Bill."

Kathy's demeanor was now as bouncy as the turbulence of the plane as it descended, even though she continued to release cleansing tears. As the flight attendant made her last rounds, she brought Kathy a tissue and asked her if she was all right. She smiled and held my hand while telling the attendant that this flight had awakened her to a renewed sense of hope.

Life is divine.

CRACKER JACKS

In my role as a medium, I find the synchronicity and divine timing of spirits to be remarkable. The greatest validation I receive from spirit is the serendipity of similar readings clustered within a short period of time. Readings for parents who have lost children, daughters who have lost mothers, clients experiencing a career change or a divorce, to name a few, commonly and magically come in bunches. I have come to learn from spirit that sitters are drawn to me by spirits with similar concerns, encouragements, or wisdom. Let me provide an example in this series of three readings that all occurred within the same day.

APRIL, JACK, AND BEN

The first reading, one cold winter morning, was over the phone. As soon as I initiated the phone call, I felt a very tall male presence, with a name that began with a "J" sound. The client, April, had said she was interested in connecting with a loved one who had recently passed. I told her I felt a tall male fatherly figure with a name that started with "J," and she confirmed that her father Jack had passed several months ago.

Jack offered the sensation that he'd passed from a disease in the chest area requiring surgery and several months of treatment. I saw a traditional heart shape in my mind, and said heart troubles. April verified that her dad had undergone open heart surgery because of leaky valves and had passed shortly after the procedure.

In my mind, I saw Jack saluting his daughter, and he was wearing a blue military uniform. Telepathically, he communicated World War II, and I saw France on a map. I could also see a red cross on his arm. April shared that both her father and she were in the Navy, and he'd often saluted her with pride. She also explained he'd been a medic in France during World War II. Jack wanted April to know he was most proud of her accomplishments as a mother and as a leader in the Navy.

Another male presented himself, standing next to Jack. He, too, was in a military uniform. I felt he was younger, funny, loved to gamble, enjoyed his cocktails and the ladies, and loved to hunt with Jack. I saw him playing horseshoes with Jack, and I sensed farmland with crops. Over the phone, I could hear a sense of relief in April's voice that her dad had found his brother Ben, who had died during the war. Although April had never met Ben, her father had often told her what a funny guy Ben was and that he loved his women. The two of them had grown up together on a farm in Iowa. April said that the night just before her reading, she'd been looking at old photos of the farm and Jack and Ben's deer hunting trips.

Ben wanted April to know he was like a godfather figure watching over her. He was pleased with her ability to organize and plan and to lead large groups of people, and pleased that she, too, wore the uniform. Jack had always told April that Ben was her guardian angel, and they both saluted her once again.

I asked April what her career was, and she said she was still a major in the Navy after many years and was getting ready to retire. She explained how much she loved both of these men and was delighted she shared the armed services experience with them.

STEVEN, JACK, AND ANTONIO

The following reading was an in-person session with a new client visiting from out of town. His name was Steven, and he was nervous about hearing something he might not want to hear from spirit. I explained that spirit only presented information that would be beneficial, encouraging, and healing to his soul. He told me two males he knew had recently passed and he would like to try to contact them.

At first, I heard the name Harry and felt the presence of a grandfather, associated with his father's side of the family. Steven told me that Harry was not actually his dad's dad, but he was the most influential man in his dad's life. I explained to Steven that a soul family extends beyond biological connections and includes those individuals who had the most impact in someone's life. Continuing with Harry's messages, I told Steven that Harry wanted him to know his father was safe with him in spirit.

A look of shock came over Steve's face as I said I could "see" a man in a green military uniform, holding a box of tools, like wrenches and screwdrivers, smoking a cigar; and I saw the name John on his name plate. John was Steven's dad, who had just passed away, and this was one of the men Steven had come to communicate with. Steven said his dad's name was actually John but everyone called him Jack, and he'd been a mechanic in the army.

In my mind, I saw a box of Cracker Jacks and asked Steven what this meant. He laughed through his tears and said his dad's nickname was Cracker Jack.

I could hear the sound of baseball on the radio and the clanking of metal tools. Also, I could smell oil and gas and saw a small garage with car hoods opened up. Steven confirmed his father owned a small body shop, and he had memories of his father listening to baseball in his shop.

Jack asked Steven to forgive him for not understanding his lifestyle and wanted him to know he loved him no matter who he spent his life with. He communicated how impressed he was with his son's ability to make the inside of a house look exceptional and homey.

Steven spoke out loud, saying he forgave his dad and was happy his dad loved him for who he was. With compassion, Jack presented a younger male who had recently passed from cancer, and he showed me the city of Seattle on a map. This younger male had a wedding ring on and he communicated that he was Steven's lover. Steven was speechless, except for saying "my Antonio." I could feel and see in his eyes his loving connection, and he commented they had met in Seattle.

Antonio offered his appreciation to Steven for allowing him to pass away at their home in their bed. He shared that he loved all the dance music at his celebration of life and acknowledged the letter that Steven had written to him. He said that he and Jack were hanging out together in spirit, getting to know each other and sharing ways to encourage and reassure Steven.

EILEEN, JACK, AND JACKY

My final reading of the day was no surprise as I connected a sitter named Eileen to a father named Jack, who was saluting an American flag in a green military uniform with lots of medals on his pocket. I could smell the fresh scent of Old Spice, which my own dad wore, and saw him shining his shoes, writing in journals on a formal desk, and eating peanuts. Eileen was so happy to identify her dad Jack, a career master sergeant in the army. She said she had to laugh about the peanuts and shining his shoes—two of his passions.

I felt the impression of heart disease and several other health issues with his digestive system. Eileen said her father had had stomach cancer, and after months of aggressive treatments, his heart had shut down. Her father shared they'd both enjoyed going to yard sales and refurnishing old wooden pieces of furniture, as Eileen nodded her head yes.

In my mind, I saw lilac and rhododendron bushes, and Eileen confirmed that her parents' backyard was filled with both of these flowering bushes. She said that many family gatherings were held in her parents' backyard, and any time she saw these flowering bushes, she thought of her parents.

To Eileen's delight, her father presented another spirit named

Jack. Telepathically, I could see the number 24. This was a muscular guy with an American flag tattoo, wearing army fatigues. I saw him with a rifle, riding in a jeep, and he presented a map of the Middle East. Over the phone, I heard a gasp from Eileen, and she said her son, who was named for her father, had passed last year in Afghanistan. She began to cry and kept repeating "my Jacky, my Jacky."

Jacky communicated that he had died overseas and was surprised how easy it was to travel into the spirit world. Although he'd never met his grandfather Jack, they instantly recognized each other in the spirit plane. In my mind, I saw a rock garden with a statue of a male angel, a small American flag, and butterflies. Eileen explained that she'd built a memory garden for both her father and son in her backyard, and a good friend had gifted her with the male statue, which reminded her of her Jacky. She created a butterfly garden and believed that when the butterflies visited, they were messages of hello from her loved ones in spirit.

In my mind, Jacky showed me a quilt in his memory, and I heard the names Jen and Grams. April was amazed that her son knew that his girlfriend Jenny and her mom had made a quilt of his clothing. He asked his mom to convey to Jenny congratulations on her new job and to tell Grams he misses her blondie brownies. Before leaving, Jacky wanted Eileen to know his black Labrador retriever was with him in spirit. It was quiet on the phone for a moment, and then Eileen said she was overwhelmed because she had had to put down Jacky's dog Coco the previous week because Coco had cancer.

Eileen was so grateful that her son and dad were together and she asked me to tell Jacky she loved him with all her heart. I explained that all she had to do was send messages within her mind, and Jack and Jacky would hear her telepathically.

Of the four readings I shared on this day, three of the readings involved Jacks with military service. It's so astounding to me how synchronistic the universe is, especially when we are working through our higher consciousness. Spirit makes it easier for me to share messages with sitters when similar circumstances and situations are presented close together. My spirit guides have reminded me that when individuals are aligned with their higher self, their I AM awareness, synchronicity and serendipity are the validation. Each week I reflect on the themes of the beautiful messages from the spirit world, and I realize an even more comprehensive meaning in the aggregate than in the individual readings themselves.

PART 3
THE SITTER

THE SITTER ~ THE RECEIVER

*"Ever has it been that love knows not its own
depth until the hour of separation."*
~ Khalil Gibran

The success of a reading has much to do with the ultimate receiver of the messages, the sitter. Personally, I encourage the sitter to be actively listening and carefully hearing what spirit has to share. I do not choose the spirits who come through for the sitter; the spirits do. The order or sequence of spirits visiting during the reading is a message to the sitter in and of itself. The current circumstances of the sitter's life help determine who will come through.

I recommend coming to a reading with an open mind and heart, and know there's more to what you feel than what you hear during the reading. Feel your loved one's presence and send appreciation and gratitude as soon as they present themselves.

Expect to be nervous and excited before speaking with the medium, but try to be at ease as much as possible to open your energy to the spiritual reading. Whether the reading is in person or on the phone, your energy will influence the perception and reception of your messages. Light a candle or incense, say a prayer, or recite inspirational literature beforehand to prepare your consciousness to experience a magical and mystical moment. Set the intention to communicate with specific loved ones in spirit, and personally invite them to the reading.

As the sitter, you are encouraged to record the session to gather information more accurately, allowing for your immediate attention to the spirit and medium. Sometimes certain information will not make sense at the moment. A recording allows you to get input from other family members. If a recording isn't possible, you're encouraged to take notes as a lot of information and messages are shared, and it will likely be difficult to remember everything. If it makes you feel more comfortable, sometimes a medium will allow a family member or friend to sit in with you during the reading. If you do bring someone to the reading, make sure the person remains silent and know that his or her loved ones in spirit might show up and present during the reading also.

Before the communication with spirit happens, I ask you, as the sitter, what you hope to achieve with the reading and if there's a certain aspect of your life for which you'd like encouragement. As the sitter, you play an important role during the reading so be attentive. *Listen carefully,* and *feel* the messages from spirit to best understand. Be aware that you may not hear what you want to hear, but it will always be in the best interest of your soul at that given moment.

Avoid interrupting the medium as much as possible, except to verify information or acknowledge a loved one. It takes great concentration to connect with your loved ones in spirit. Expect there to be spaces of silence during the reading, as the medium receives the subtle information and must carefully listen and perceive. Try not to fill in information unless the medium asks you to provide insight.

Often, I have found the sitter to be overwhelmed when loved ones visit and present touching messages. Expect the reading to heighten your emotions, and know that it truly is a magical and mystical experience when spirit visits. It's all right if you don't know or understand the information right away. Often, I find sitters having psychic amnesia, forgetting little details about a loved one.

Your loved ones in spirit will communicate subtle but specific pieces of information that will be helpful if you are aware and actively engaged. Again, listen carefully to the messages. You may ask certain spirits to come to the reading ahead of time, but be flexible and understanding about who comes through during the reading. I can only deliver to the sitter what spirit is willing to share with me.

Sit with the information from your reading for several days and it will start to have greater meaning. Share the information with family members who may be able to validate certain information you aren't aware of or have forgotten. If something still doesn't make sense, know that it might be something or someone coming to you in the future.

If other family members get a reading, different spirits might show up or they may come in a different sequence. The evidential information presented may vary from the same spirit because spirits use evidence specific to the sitter, and sitters have had different experiences and perceptions. The most important knowledge to receive as a sitter is that life is continuous beyond the death of the physical body, and your love will be forever with your loved ones.

Celebrate the spiritual reading with loving kindness. Accept those spirits who want to ask for forgiveness, offer supportive advice, and encourage choices that bring more peace and happiness to your life.

Seeing is believing is only relevant when you choose to limit your perspective to the physical world. *Believing is seeing* is much more relevant to sensing and experiencing the energies of the spiritual world and beyond. As you believe, so shall you perceive.

I CAN HEAR YOU

For several years, Sherri harbored much grief after the sudden passing of her son Aidan and several other close family members. As part of the process to soothe her sorrow, she reluctantly tried several mediums to connect to spirit. The readings comforted her for only a brief time. One rainy morning, she felt her son guided her to his computer, and she was intuitively led to my website. Still reluctant, she scheduled a reading.

On the day of her phone reading, I introduced myself and explained the way in which I use my higher consciousness to blend with spirit. At first I felt the presence of a grandfather on Sherri's father's side and sensed he had passed at his work from a sudden heart attack. I saw cleaning supplies and felt I was in a large building. Sherri confirmed that her grandfather was a janitor in a factory and he passed from a heart attack while he was cleaning one day at work. Pappy, as she called him, said he was a guardian to Sherri, and he loved that she had followed her passion and gotten a teaching degree after he passed.

Pappy acknowledged that his son, Sherri's father, was in spirit with him. Frank communicated that he had loved working in the garage on engines and had been an avid motorcyclist. He shared that he had died when Sherri was a child and that she kept a photo of the two of them sitting on his Harley by a lake.

Sherri validated that her father passed on a motorcycle when she was four, and the only memory she had was the photo of them on his bike by the lake. Frank communicated that their love was everlasting and he appreciated that she still prayed to him every night. He knew of her recent loss and had been providing signs of his presence with the song "Stairway to Heaven" and other Led Zeppelin songs that she often came across when feeling strong grief.

Frank also told his daughter during the reading that he had a younger male with him in spirit, and both Pappy and he wanted to gift her with a visit from him. The younger male presented himself in a purple hoodie and with a skateboard in his hands. He kept using his hands to make two gestures, like some type of code. As I explained them to Sherri, she was astonished. It turns out, I was signing the letters "A" and "J," and Sherri was so surprised I heard the phone drop. She explained that her son AJ was in spirit, and he had been deaf. He often wore his favorite color purple, and he was an excellent skateboarder. Even though I could mentally hear him, he wanted to validate his name to his mom using sign language. AJ communicated that Pappy and Frank were with him in spirit, and they enjoyed many times together fishing.

It brought Sherri great comfort knowing that her son was with Pappy and that he shared reliable evidence to help her overcome her sense of loss. AJ shared that he'd been hit by a car and his mom hadn't had time to get to the hospital before he passed. He again showed me a series of three hand gestures that Sherri recognized as "I love ya." AJ wanted me to tell his mom to please not feel guilty for not being there when he passed. He said it was much easier to go without saying goodbye, and Pappy and Frank were there to meet him.

AJ explained to his mom that he could hear her; he could hear what was in her heart. He thanked her for being so helpful to so many other children with disabilities. Sherri told me that she had become a special education teacher after Pappy and AJ passed, and that she specialized in teaching hearing impaired children. AJ also let his mom know he had loved to work with hearing impaired children while he was here on the earth plane, and he still enjoyed helping children who passed over to spirit. Although he said there was no need for physical communication in spirit, he enjoyed mastering the art of communicating with his mom, his brother, and his grandmas, who were still in the earth plane.

A few years after her first reading, Sherri scheduled another reading. Again, she was blessed with visits from all three men. They continued to validate the signs and symbols they put in her path to let her know they were with her. She explained to me after the reading that she had had her mother and mother-in-law schedule readings with me the previous year. Most of the information was quite similar, she said, but there were a few differences.

One specific message that came through to her mother, Sherri explained, was most helpful to AJ's brother, Josh. Sherri's mom Angela had a phone reading and was confused about how the process worked. She didn't confirm information or participate in the reading at all. Information came through from her family members, but she was so anxious she didn't say anything.

AJ visited his grandma during her reading, and he identified himself with a purple and gray hooded sweatshirt, which she'd given him for his last Christmas. He also communicated how much he'd loved her homemade waffles and had enjoyed the times they built a patio and garden in the backyard. Angela wanted the evidence that her daughter Sherri had received, about AJ being deaf. As a medium, I present the information that's given to me, and I was not told or shown AJ's disability during grandma's reading. In fact, I only knew this spirit as a grandson with the name Aidan, who wanted to communicate memories specific to his experience with his grandma. Angela called her grandson Aidan and she hadn't learned sign language as Sherri had.

The one critical message from Aidan that Angela remembered, though, was to help his brother Josh. He shared that Josh was deeply depressed but kept it hidden. During the reading, he showed me Josh was a cutter. He would cut his upper arm, hoping to distract himself from the emotional pain, and kept it hidden from the family. Angela also learned that Josh was extremely frightened of losing other family members and didn't want to drive for fear of hitting another person because this was how his brother had been killed. Josh even had panic attacks just riding in the car.

Weeks after her mom's reading, Sherri told me they were able to talk with Josh about his fears. The message from AJ saved his life because Josh had been planning to commit suicide from the grief of losing his brother. AJ (Aidan) was acting as a guardian, providing messages to his family so his brother could be saved. Now Josh was receiving professional help.

When our loved ones in spirit communicate with loving kindness, there are no boundaries or barriers. Our spirit family members share their expansive awareness, gracious thanks, and continuous communications with us all. Their messages are specific to each family member according to the experiences they shared. The waffles and garden were treasured moments with Grandma Angela, while skateboarding and signing were more associated with his mom Sherri.

I'm still amazed that AJ was able to get through to me using sign language and to help his family from the spirit world. Our loved ones in spirit truly are connected to us and support us in the physical plane. I appreciate how clever and innovative they can be in sharing messages with loved ones. We are so blessed.

THE CLOUDY STAR

I was more nervous than normal to read for a famous television star, but I was determined to allow my intuition to connect and bring through messages that would benefit the person the most. As I picked up the phone to call, I felt a sense of challenges coming my way.

After I introduced myself and explained how my mental mediumship worked, I asked if she had any questions. She said she had specific things she wanted to inquire about, and I explained I would like the opportunity to connect with her loved ones in spirit first. Then I would provide time for her questions. She reluctantly agreed and I began my service to spirit.

Initially, I sensed the presence of a tall lady with white hair. She was well dressed, seemed quite proper and educated, and had a grandmother-like vibration. I sensed she had a connection to the theater because I saw her on a stage in my mind. I heard the name Elsie, and the sitter confirmed that this was her maternal grandmother, but her name was Elsa. The sitter then said she wasn't interested in Grandma and asked what color dress she should wear to receive her Emmy.

I explained I wasn't a psychic but that Grandma Elsa, in spirit, could help with advice and encouragement for the sitter's career. Elsa encouraged her granddaughter to pursue a local college film project to get special recognition and develop her screen presence. I saw in my mind that the project was a historic piece and more of a documentary than a regular film. The sitter said she didn't need advice about her career because she had an agent for that. She reiterated that, instead, she wanted to know what dress she should wear to receive her television award.

As I more strongly blended with Elsa, I did not see the sitter receiving an award, at least at this time, but I explained that if she followed her grandma's advice, she would be offered other and better opportunities. Elsa asked me to relay that a particular onstage theater project in Seattle would be helpful to the sitter's career. Grandma wanted to help her granddaughter achieve success, and she explained that receiving awards is only a small aspect of it. Achievement, she conveyed, comes with using your talent in many different situations and by playing diverse characters.

The sitter became agitated and demanded that I move on to another topic because I obviously couldn't read her correctly in regards to her Emmy. I was thinking, why am I subjecting myself to this? But I do love a challenge, especially when it involves helping another soul see things from a higher perspective. I reassured the sitter that Grandma Elsa loves her very much and will be available to help her with her career, if she is open to receive insights.

At that point, I heard the very loud presence of a Billy and felt he was a rebel and father-like energy. He asked me to say hello to the sitter, and she confirmed that this was her "loser" father. Through me, Billy apologized for not being a good dad, and avowed that he was learning how to control his temper and addictive personality. He asked his daughter to be open to listen to and take in the messages because he didn't want her to be unhappy and miserable, as he had been when he was in the earth plane.

The sitter requested that I tell her about the new television show contract she had signed. I asked Billy to help me understand, and I saw the contract being put in a drawer and locked away. I also saw a blank television screen and felt there would be no show at this time. Now, I don't enjoy being the messenger for disappointing news, but I must exhibit integrity and honor regarding what spirit shows me. Billy told me to tell his daughter that the show would be on hold for now, but other opportunities in theater were available to her, as Grandma Elsa had communicated.

Immediately, the sitter yelled at me over the phone and told me I didn't know what I was saying. I calmly explained I had to provide the insights I was given, which doesn't mean I'm always right. But I was thinking to myself that it felt very right. The sitter commented that I obviously was unable to clearly and accurately provide insight about her career, so she asked if I would address her love life. As I tell all my clients, I told her I could help her understand what emotional or mental obstacles she might have that could be preventing a relationship, or a kindhearted relationship, but I couldn't predict the future.

The sitter provided me with the name Larry and asked me if I saw him as her soul mate. She said many psychics have told her that the two of them would be together forever, as romantic lovers.

As I tuned into the situation, I felt a warm, nurturing presence and, in my mind, I saw this person doing needlepoint in a rocking chair. I communicated that this grandma-like energy was very loving and had known the sitter as a little girl. I could see this spirit helping the sitter dance in front of a mirror, and I also saw the spirit teaching the sitter how to act.

I heard a long sigh, and the sitter said this must be Dorothy, the dance and acting teacher she'd had for years when she was a young lady. She said Dorothy also taught her how to sew her own costumes.

Dorothy was exceedingly kindhearted and communicated that she cared about the well-being of the sitter. She told me to share with the sitter that Larry was not available emotionally. I could see a wedding ring on his finger and shared this information. The sitter was not at all happy when Dorothy reminded her (through me) that Larry was, in fact, married. I also saw two children with Larry, and the sitter confirmed that he did have two children.

Next, Dorothy showed me a calendar with the month of January circled, and on a map, she showed me New York City. With a sense of intrigue, the sitter verified that the last time she'd spoken with Larry was in January, eight months earlier, and he'd been in New

York City. I thanked Dorothy for sharing these details so we could both help awaken the sitter to the reality of things. I explained that Dorothy was helping her to understand that Larry was not an option at this time.

Dorothy also communicated that she wanted her former student to be at peace with herself and to love herself completely. She asked her to reflect on the messages provided so she would know her loved ones in spirit were supporting her efforts, but that, ultimately, her own choices were causing her pain and suffering.

The sitter was extremely angry with me because a number of psychics had told her she would win an Emmy that year, she would have a successful television show, and Larry would leave his wife and children to be her soul mate. I asked the sitter to please be encouraged by the loved ones who visited with her and to find gratitude for their messages. She called me some lower vibrational names and demanded I refund her money. I explained that I had provided the services I promised, and I wished her peace. She hung up.

This was an immensely important lesson for me as an intuitive medium, which is why I shared this reading with you. It might be easy to tell people what they want to hear, but is that being loving and supportive? As a reader, I don't ever want to facilitate fear within another person or provide false hope.

I also wanted to share this story because, to me, it was one of the most amazing connections I've made, with specific details and wise information for the sitter. Spirit knows what's in our best interest— what can best serve the progression our soul has come to the physical plane to work through, and what issues we came to heal.

Upon reflecting on this reading, I more fully realized I can't take credit for the astute messages shared through a reading from spirit; I am simply the messenger.

One year later, the same sitter asked for another reading because she was still interested in knowing about her award, television show, and love life. I decided it was best for her to speak with another medium, and I hoped that her loved ones would help her see things from a fresh perspective so she could find happiness and peace of mind.

BIRDIES

Depending on which family member is receiving a reading, their loved ones in spirit employ different signs and symbols, offering comparable themes. The magnitude of their ingenuity can be demonstrated by the various levels of meaning in this story about the birdies. The family members involved in this reading experienced the tragedy of both a father and a son committing suicide by hanging themselves.

John Jr., or JJ, took his own life on a cold January day by hanging himself in the garage, just two years after his father had done so. His mind was clouded with unhinged panic and exhausting fear. His suffering didn't end when his spirit left his physical shell, but his perspective shifted. Without the heaviness and judgment of the ego-mind, his soul went into a cocoon state of self-reflection. Each soul experiences a life review and feels all the emotions and thoughts they created through personal choice in relation to their soul family members. Soul family members include any souls from your biological family, adopted family, or friendships who are closely connected to similar karma and soul agreements.

As JJ's soul was completing his life review, his family members in the earth plane were in a state of shock, guilt, and then grief and anger. JJ inspired them telepathically to get professional help and spiritual consultation. He was unaware he could communicate with them through a medium.

Debra, John's widow, was the first family member to reach out for a reading. My parents knew Debra through their golf league, and she overheard them talking about incredible messages from some of my recent readings. She scheduled a reading when I was home visiting family for the Christmas holiday.

Initially, a fatherly spirit presented to Debra, and he showed me the letter "J" and a white van associated with his work. I could smell cigarette smoke and sensed he was a heavy smoker, and I saw him sitting at a restaurant counter with coffee, ham, and eggs, reading the newspaper.

Smiling, Debra validated this must be her father-in-law, who like his son, was named John. She said every morning he used to order ham and eggs and read their horoscopes from the newspaper as she served him at the diner where she waitressed. I felt he had rough hands from working with tools. Debra confirmed she didn't remember ever seeing him without a cigarette in his mouth, and he'd been a builder and painter.

In my mind, John showed me coins, and Debra laughed because John often left her pennies and nickels as a comical tip. She also acknowledged she often found change in strange locations, such as on her car seat, the kitchen counter, and the floor in the den, or in her favorite rocking chair and many other uncommon locations. Coins are a constant reminder to value yourself, John communicated to his favorite daughter-in-law.

John apologized for leaving the earth plane so quickly by taking his own life and for not leaving a letter to explain. He asked Debra to tell his wife to accept his apology. His depression had overcome him and he just couldn't be in the physical anymore. He requested she pass on the message that he loved his wife dearly and missed her meatloaf and chunky mashed potatoes. He also asked Debra to tell her he was often sitting in the recliner he'd napped in after work.

With tears, Debra listened patiently for every little message he shared. He then said he wanted to bring his son and her husband, John Jr., through, as they were together in the spirit plane. John showed me a visual of the two of them on the golf course, and he said his son was the messenger of all the "birdies." "Please be assured,"

John told Debra, "that I was there to greet him on his transition to spirit."

John Jr. was very reluctant to communicate with me at first because, as a new spirit, he didn't know he could come through to us. In my mind, I saw him with his head down, in a white T-shirt and white pants, holding buckets filled with rollers and paintbrushes. He was quite short and muscular, and had scruffy red hair. Debra cried and confirmed this description fit her husband JJ, who'd been a painter like his father.

John Jr., or JJ, communicated that he'd been in spirit only a short time, and I sensed his shame and embarrassment for his method of crossing. JJ impressed in my mind that he'd felt hopeless with his relationships and grief and guilt from the passing of his father. I felt he couldn't breathe and that one of his sons had come home just after he'd hung himself. Debra cried and said that her youngest son had come home from school to find the lifeless body of his dad in the garage.

JJ showed me golf clubs and a cooler of beer, and I could hear heavy metal music playing. He communicated that he missed their friends in the golf league and asked Debra to say "hey" to Dennis and Charlie and to please thank them for helping out the boys and her. Nodding with tears, Debra said these were two of several of his golf besties, and they had been spending extra time with their three boys.

Debra asked how she would know when JJ is with her. I immediately saw a cardinal and heard JJ say he wanted to bring happiness and joy to her for how kind she'd been to him and how loving she was to the boys. Pulling up her sleeve, Debra showed me she'd gotten a cardinal tattoo on her forearm in his memory. She often saw two cardinals together and JJ conveyed that he and his dad were showing up together as the cardinals. As soon as I said this, a bright red cardinal landed on the window ledge next to our chairs. With a look of awe, I explained to Debra how much JJ and John wanted us to know they were present for the reading. Nature provides unique opportunities to send signs to those we love in the earth plane, JJ communicated. Debra and I continued to smile with tears in our eyes.

Debra purchased a reading for her mother-in-law for Christmas, and I met with her on my return visit to my hometown that summer. Mable used to be a bright-spirited, jolly lady until the loss of both her husband and son to suicide in the past several years. Her face was etched with deep lines of grief. She was reluctant to get a reading, but I assured her it may help her have a deeper understanding about her life and her connection to those she loved in spirit.

The first spirit to communicate with us had a mother-like vibration and I heard the name Doris. Before I finished my sentence, Mable exclaimed that her dear mother Doris was there. Doris had a strong vibration of motherly kindheartedness and showed me her passion to knit and crochet. In my mind, I saw a blue and green afghan, lots of sweaters neatly folded with images of birds on them, and a big round basket holding ribbons, balls of yarn, and knitting needles. Knitting was Doris's lifelong passion and Mable explained that she knitted each of her grandchildren sweaters with ducks and birds on them because they all loved nature.

I then saw hummingbirds on a sweater, and in my mind, I could see many hummingbird feeders. Mable smiled and said her mother had crafted a sweater with hummingbirds, and she remembered her mom had several feeders just outside her windows. "Please be at peace in your heart," Doris communicated to her daughter. "I am looking out for your boys in spirit. The hummingbirds are signs that your boys are healing and sending you love." With a look of wonderment, Mable smiled and said she often saw hummingbirds sitting on her wire fence when she gardened in the backyard.

A husband vibration now presented himself, as I clairvoyantly saw a wedding band; and on a calendar, I saw Christmas Day circled twice. Mable began to cry and said that her husband John was in spirit, and they had been married on Christmas. John jokingly communicated that he had to get married on a day she wouldn't forget, and Mable said, "That's my John."

She begged to know why he left so suddenly and what she could have done to make him happier. I sensed a strong sense of guilt from John's spirit, and John admitted his extreme use of alcohol to try to escape from his melancholy. He asked me to tell Mable that if it weren't for her dependable love and support, he would have left many years ago. "Please forgive me and know that I'm spending time with our son in spirit," he conveyed. "Junior is here with me, Mom," (as he often called Mable, she said) "and together we're figuring things out and learning how to govern our minds with virtuous intentions."

Next, JJ (John Jr.) presented and validated himself as a painter with a passion for golf and the father of three boys. Most important, he wanted to let his mom know how much he loved her. He also wanted to express his appreciation for all the special things she'd done to make him feel treasured, such as helping him start his painting business, teaching him how to golf, and cooking his favorite spaghetti dinner every Sunday. JJ assured his mom he would watch out for his three sons but was most concerned about Luke, his youngest son. He showed me bags full of empty whiskey bottles and his son alone, sitting in darkness, depressed and scared.

The third member of the family to get a reading was Luke, because Mable and Debra were both concerned about the message from JJ about Luke's drinking problem and depression. The following fall I met with Luke, and he requested that his mom Debra be present because he was both skeptical and nervous. Luke told me he had heard about his relatives coming through in a reading, but he wasn't sure if he believed in an afterlife. He said he didn't feel he deserved to have anyone visit him.

Immediately, a father figure with the name John (JJ) once again presented himself as a painter and lover of hunting and golf. Hesitantly, Luke confirmed that he and his father had golfed and hunted together when he was younger and that he'd helped his dad with his painting business. JJ showed me a lawn mower, hedge clippers, and a wheel barrel. I telepathically heard JJ say to his son to "follow your passion with yard work." Luke looked confused because he thought his father would have wanted him to maintain his business painting houses. Luke explained that he loved doing landscaping and had often considered changing his work.

With a heavy heart, JJ communicated he was very sorry Luke had found him in the garage when he passed. He conveyed to his son that he'd learned he couldn't escape his depression or surrender his dark thoughts. Luke cried and said he often thought about suicide because he was miserable with his life. JJ wanted Luke to understand it was important for them both to release the idea they weren't good enough and that no one cared. He asked Luke to engage in the family's Methodist church to search for his Higher Power.

JJ impressed an image of a bulldog in my mind, and I asked Luke if he had a dog in spirit. He explained that he had one dog here and one had died shortly after his father had passed. Clairvoyantly I saw B and B, and Luke said their names were Bach and Beethoven because he liked classical music. I conveyed that his dad had one of the dogs there with him, and Luke was relieved to know that Bach was with his father. I saw Bach with a gray rubber toy like a dinosaur, and Luke said that was close; it was a rhinoceros, and Bach had been buried with it.

Within my mind, I saw golf clubs and heard JJ say to think of him as a caddy to Luke throughout his life. Dad acknowledged how the two of them had often golfed together and that Luke held the course record for most birdies in a season. Luke smiled for the first time during his reading and said he'd broken his own father's birdie record, and that he often saw crows on the golf course. JJ conveyed that the crows, hummingbirds, and cardinals were all birdies, and symbolically, he wanted his loved ones to know he was flying high above his problems and that he'd found a sense of freedom from his depression. "The birdies are *me* sending you all my well wishes and love," JJ communicated.

OPEN HEARTED

For many years, Maria harbored a sense of separation and sadness from grieving the loss of the love of her life. She believed there must be life after death, but being a scientist, she often overanalyzed everything. She learned about meditation through practicing yoga and started to align more with her feelings.

In time, Maria would often sense she needed to visit Palm Springs and be open to whatever spiritual messages she received, in whatever form she received them. She didn't know why she was called to the desert from the ocean, but she followed her strong insights and visited Palm Springs.

Maria was drawn to a specific yoga studio, and after a relaxing class, she saw a flyer on the door of the yoga studio that stated a local medium was offering a demonstration that very night at the studio. The owner of the studio provided one of my business cards, and when Maria learned I was a cell and molecular biologist, similar to her, she decided to come to the presentation.

At the event, Maria's mother came forth and provided specific evidence, communicating they had the same name, and that she was from the Chicago area. Her mom also stated that she'd had Alzheimer's and that Maria had a sister who had cared for her. She asked Maria not to feel guilty for not quitting her job and moving back home. Maria's analytical mind was impressed with the quick reading, but she was wondering why her husband hadn't come through. She asked for a one-on-one reading after the demonstration, and we met a few days later.

Upon arriving for her reading, Maria reminded me she'd been at the recent demonstration and that she'd only been to a card reader and psychics before. She admitted she was quite skeptical but was open to see who might visit her during her reading.

I explained to her that a psychic is a person who has a higher sensitivity than usual to the energies within and around a person. Mediums are psychics, but they receive most of their information from communication with members of the sitter's soul family who have crossed into spirit.

Maria asked if her soul family included just the relatives she knew here in her life. I explained that a soul family consists of ancestors, family members, work associates, and close friends who share a common soul purpose. Soul family members are telepathically linked to one another and are working through similar karma. As each soul family member develops spiritually, they contribute to the entire family. Because souls are interconnected, even souls you have not met physically but who are linked to someone you love belong to the same soul family. This is why loved ones in spirit stay in touch; you help them evolve as they help you evolve.

I enjoy when spirit comes through to help me emphasize a point. For Maria, her mother-in-law came through, and she said she had never met Maria but she appreciated the care Maria had given to Rob, her son, who was also in spirit. Maria smiled because her husband Bob had told Maria that his mom called him Rob, but everyone else called him Bob.

Bob needed the assistance of his mom to communicate because he told me he had only been in spirit for a short time, and he wanted to make sure it was all right to speak with me. Rob-Bob communicated through his mom that he had had cancer and hadn't appreciated his Buddha belly, which developed with the inflammation in his abdomen. Maria confirmed that Bob had always been lean, but his lymphoma had caused his belly to bloat toward the end of his life.

I could taste licorice in my mouth and Bob conveyed that he'd loved to snack on licorice and graham crackers. Maria laughed because every week she'd bought him red licorice as a treat, and when they watched movies on the couch at night, he'd always want graham crackers.

In my mind, I saw Bob carrying a briefcase and sitting at a desk with many books behind him. He communicated that he'd been a leader in his field of work, spent many hours at his desk, and loved history. Maria explained that he'd been a high school history teacher and then had become the school's principal.

Bob then mentally shared blueprints with me, and I heard him state he was disappointed he didn't get to be here long enough to see the completion of the buildings. Maria gasped and said that he had had a goal to complete a new gym and library at the high school, but he'd become ill and passed before the new buildings were completed. Bob said to communicate that he was flattered that his name went in the room with all the bookshelves. Maria acknowledged that the school dedicated the reading room of the new library to Bob.

Maria asked Bob what he missed the most. From the perspective of a spirit, Bob explained that they don't miss things like we do because they realize the eternal connection to everything and everybody. He did show me trips to the Eiffel Tower, and Maria validated that they had taken many trips to their favorite city, Paris.

Next, Bob communicated that he wanted to thank his good friend, an accountant who often golfed with him and had known Bob since his teenage years. He also said this friend had spoken nicely about him at his funeral. Maria shared that Paul was Bob's dearest friend and she acknowledged the information presented about Paul.

Maria asked me to see what Bob thought she should do with the rest of her life. He encouraged her to continue the winter trips to the desert and Maui and to start painting her abstract oil paintings again. Tearing up, Maria validated their annual trips to these locations and said she hadn't painted since Bob was diagnosed with cancer several years ago.

Bob then mentally impressed in my mind an image of rocks in the shape of a heart, which I shared with Maria. With a look of shock and awe, Maria said she'd made a heart-shaped rock formation with stones she brought on each visit to his grave. Bob shared that the Fourth of July was extra special to him. Through joyful tears, Maria told me the Fourth was their wedding anniversary. He let her know she didn't need to go to the cemetery every day because he would always be within her heart. Maria was overjoyed with all the evidence that Bob shared with her during the reading, but her mind still struggled to believe that Bob remained with her. One more time, she skeptically asked me to inquire of Bob how she could be sure he was nearby.

Mentally, Bob transmitted an image of a crystal vase with pink baby roses next to the bed. I also saw a bag of red licorice on a pillow. Maria jumped out of her chair and hugged me. She explained that Bob used to bring her a pink rose every week and since he passed, she keeps a vase of them near her bed. She also told me that because Bob loved red licorice so much, she leaves a bag of it on his pillow. She was now convinced that Bob was with her and felt great relief from her reading.

Maria realized that Bob and her mom must have helped her to find me. Since Maria and I had similar scientific backgrounds, we shared an analytical perspective and could easily relate to each other for a reading. Coming to a reading with no expectations and an open mind and heart will inspire mystical and meaningful messages from loved ones in spirit.

NIGHTMARE TO PARADISE

There is no greater pleasure than witnessing the progression of a person from self-punishment, shame, and dark sadness to a forgiving, flexible, and easy-going optimism with the assistance from loved ones in spirit. Ned has been a client of mine for over ten years and has freely trusted me to provide messages that have changed his perspective about himself and life.

For Ned's first reading, he secretly drove via a back road because his family had strong religious beliefs that to communicate with the dead was the work of Satan. He was a well-respected and successful financial genius and the CFO of a large corporation in Cleveland, Ohio. Ned could increase capital and reduce expenditures to create profits unheard of, and he lived comfortably in a mansion with all the luxuries of a corporate king.

He answered the phone with a nervous voice and was reluctant to respond to questions or provide feedback. At first, I clairvoyantly saw a large man dressed in a three-piece suit and carrying an attaché case. I saw the letter "F" and Ned quietly replied that that sounded like his father-in-law Fredrick. Fredrick showed me business cards and communicated that they worked together, which Ned confirmed. I saw accountant ledgers, images of stocks and bonds, and Fredrick sitting at a desk in a skyscraper.

I felt heaviness in the lungs and lots of coughing and smelled cigarettes. Ned said that Fredrick had recently passed away from lung cancer and had been a heavy smoker. Fredrick was pleased with how well the business was doing and congratulated Ned for all his efforts. More important, though, Fredrick shared an insight: Although he had enjoyed all the riches and recognition that came with the success of the business, he wished he had spent more time with his family.

Now I was drawn to a nurturing motherly vibration and I felt she had passed from a stroke or trauma to the head, which caused her to be paralyzed and unable to speak. I saw the letter "A" embroidered on a lacey handkerchief. Ned was astonished that his Grandma Ann, who raised him as her own, came to visit. During his senior year of college, Ned said Ann had a stroke and passed before he could return home because he had final exams.

Ann reassured Ned that she harbored no ill will for him not coming home. I could smell cinnamon coffee cake and saw a cast iron pan with breakfast cooking. Ned replied that he still had his grandma's pan and her recipe for coffee cake. Ann wanted Ned to know that she prayed for him to overcome his grief from his most recent losses. She brought through a spirit dressed in an Army uniform, and he took off his hat to bow to Ned. He showed me that he had had stomach problems and had been hospitalized for many weeks before he passed. He thanked Ned for coming to see him almost every day when he was ill.

Ned responded that this was his brother Harry, a career army lieutenant, who had passed from stomach cancer. Harry assured Ned that he was all right and was reviewing his life in the spirit plane. He told his little brother not to work so hard and to enjoy himself and encouraged him to explore the castles and cathedrals of Great Britain. He also thanked Ned for arranging his funeral and for contacting his son, with whom he hadn't spoken during the last ten years of his life.

Ned didn't say much on the other end of the phone, but I asked him if this all made sense. He said yes, but he wanted to hear from one more person—his son.

In my mind, I saw a boy packing his bags for college with math and science books in his backpack and a pair of running shoes. I felt he was ambitious and friendly. Ned confirmed that his son had been an engineering major and had run college track. I saw a tall lanky boy with red hair and freckles and the letter "C." Ned said his name was Connor.

Connor communicated how much he appreciated spending time hiking and camping with his dad when he was in grade school. I could hear Ned begin to cry, and then weep—a strong cleansing cry he'd suppressed for over sixteen months. There was a moment when I felt the father and son connected, and it appeared to be the beginning of a genuine healing.

Connor wished me to tell his dad that he'd been foolish to take his own life because of his fears of not being successful and the pressure of trying to be perfect. Connor said he was meditating and doing lots of self-reflection in spirit to understand the pain and suffering he caused others and to forgive himself for having so many expectations.

Ned interrupted with great intensity and sobbed, saying, "Please ask Connor to forgive me for pressuring him and for not being around much during his high school years."

Connor communicated that he took full responsibility for his actions but asked his father to make sure he considered having a more relaxed approach to his life. In my mind, I saw beautiful mountains, lakes, rivers, and forests, and Connor said to tell his dad to go heal in nature.

Ned asked his son how he could best help his mom with her grief. Connor said his mom didn't want to talk about him anymore, and she was ignoring her feelings. He believed she would suffer in silence, but he encouraged his dad to tell her of their communication today.

Every year on Connor's birthday, Ned would schedule a reading to connect with his son. I felt they both learned so much from each other, and together they healed and learned to surrender their fears and embrace the little and meaningful gifts from heaven.

Throughout all these readings, various friends and relatives would stop in from the spirit world to offer messages, and Ned asked why the same spirits didn't always come through. I explained what my spirit guides told me: Spirits come through during a reading according to what's going on in the consciousness of the sitter at that time and what healing and information would be of greatest help. Certain loved ones in spirit are better suited than others to help with relationships, family matters, career challenges, or health matters, for example. Also, spirits have tasks to complete related to their own healing and the enlightenment they seek, so they're not always available to visit during a reading.

Every time I read for Ned, his son Connor and his Grandma Ann were eager to share communications, but they provided a variety of messages according to what Ned was experiencing in his life at the time. Through their wise council, Ned learned that he was responsible for the conditions of his life, and these conditions were based on his choices. During readings, he often asked for his son's and grandma's advice, and they consistently provided fresh perspectives but never made the choice for Ned. Ned learned that his free will was an ultimate ally and he was able to consider the wise guidance from his loved ones in spirit to bring more peace and joy into his life.

After eight years of phone readings, Ned decided to travel to one of my workshops and meet me for a reading in person. He was quite scared and felt guilty about many new choices he was making to change his life. Connor came through to communicate that he loved his dad's new shack, especially the pine paneling. Ned laughed, but this was one area where he felt guilty. He explained he had decided to leave his wife because he couldn't handle not being able to talk and express his feelings about the passing of his son and many other things. In my mind, I saw a small porch, shelves of books, a small wooden desk with a journal, and lots of pine trees. Ned explained that he'd taken Connor's desk and was doing automatic writing and journaling. His new home in the woods was quite humble, and he often sat on the porch thinking of Connor.

Ned asked his loved ones in spirit if he'd done the right thing by leaving his job and his wife to find happiness. As soon as he asked, two hummingbirds came up to the picture widow in the office and just hovered there for a minute. Tears ran down Ned's face and he explained that he saw hummingbirds as a sign of both his son and grandma. I told Ned that hummingbirds are believed to be the bringers of joy in Native American culture. His answers were right in front of his face.

Ned had never taken a vacation from his work or family, and his travels here to the workshop and reading demonstrated his commitment to make changes in his life, as communicated by his Grandma Ann. His grandma conveyed that Ned was very brave and that the oneness and attitude of gratitude and appreciation Ned gifted himself was beneficial to his own healing.

As I sat with Ned, I realized the remarkable progression he'd made in his life, which had been filled with unexpected obstacles—but obstacles that helped him to know himself. Ned experienced the darkest depression from the loss of a child and then separation from his career and his wife. These changes turned out to be gifts to help him understand the truths of life. His loved ones communicated how proud they were of him for all he'd done to transform his life and accomplish his greatest achievement: inner peace.

PART 4

THE SPIRIT

THE SPIRIT ~ THE SENDER

"Death in the physical is the birth in the spiritual. Birth in the physical is death in the spiritual." ~ Edgar Cayce

A medium works on behalf of your loved ones in spirit by providing a means to present their messages with precision and commitment. The aptitude and level of consciousness of the medium can influence the message, but ultimately, spirit has the highest (literally) ability to control the content and communications of a reading.

On many levels, your loved ones in spirit can guide you to a specific medium they feel can most effectively communicate their messages. Intuitively, spirit can do this by providing you with an insight or a feeling about a certain medium, or they might inspire a friend or relative to tell you about someone.

Once a reading begins, your loved ones have a "knowing" as to which of them can convey their messages with the most accurate information and trust to the medium. Spirit also knows what issues and concerns require the most attention and/or guidance for the sitter and which messages would be most comforting and supportive.

Your loved ones in the spirit world have distinct roles in support and encouragement for each sitter at certain times and for specific situations. For example, a grandma might be most helpful with family advice, a father or mother might give useful career counsel, or a good friend in spirit might best provide insight regarding your soul's path.

The sequence in which loved ones in spirit present themselves is a message in itself. Many times, a spirit will want to present another loved one in spirit to reinforce the notion that family members stay connected to one another even in the spirit world.

Spirits are also inclined to masterfully reinforce messages in a reading by the chronological order in which they present themselves. As you can see from many of the readings in this book, your loved ones in spirit present themselves according to what is most significant to your life experience at the time of your reading. For example, if you're having difficulties with your career, certain loved ones will provide support and professional counsel, depending on the most appropriate spirit to do so. If you have health challenges of great importance, then a loved one whose knowledge, expertise, or relationship is relevant may present valuable insight regarding your well-being. Perhaps you're grieving the recent loss of a partner. A specific spirit may present to advise you on your state of mind, or loved ones of your partner who are also in spirit may communicate to let you know they were there to greet the deceased and provide comfort. Therefore, the messenger him- or herself can also be a message.

A seasoned medium is able to provide specific evidence you can personally associate with your loved one in spirit. Each spirit works independently and might give his or her name, a letter of the name, a specific month, an occupation, hobby, or passion, a specific location, or an activity you enjoyed together. Once you've identified the spirit, take a moment to feel his or her presence. The energy of the spirit is very strong during a reading.

The most important aspect of a reading is the encouragement, inspiration, or words of enlightenment that your loved ones share with you. Within the higher plane of spirit, your loved ones have an enormous change in perspective. They have a higher, more expansive view of life and therefore can provide wise and objective insights about your life issues.

I've found that spirit is excellent at helping sitters perceive and remove the emotional obstacles of fear and guilt as well as the mental barriers of judgment and doubt. Also, spirit can impress intuitive insights upon the mind of the sitter or provide guidance through the medium or in a dream. In these ways, spirit can convey to an individual how to best rectify situations and overcome obstacles, and inspire choices on how to approach karmic debt and progress the soul.

We are so blessed to have the unique vision and loving kindness of spirits in a higher realm. When a spirit leaves the physical body, the individual has a much more expansive vision and a remembrance of the eternal and divine self. The higher self knows and understands far beyond the limits of the ego-mind.

Our loved ones in spirit have free will as to whether or not they will communicate. They determine if they feel comfortable communicating with a specific medium and if the sitter is open to receive a specific message. Also, they might not always be available to communicate during a specific reading. They have responsibilities to heal and grow as well as obligations to serve the world of spirit in various capacities. For example, spirits help one another with their life reviews, observing and sharing their karmic lessons, and help orient spirits new to the spirit plane. They fulfill lessons of the soul, karma, and soul families, and learn how to bring peace, joy, and more understanding to their consciousness, just to name a few of their tasks. With that level of understanding, never doubt their unending encouragement and loving reassurance.

Spirits communicate with one another and can thus obtain "referrals" to a medium who has had success communicating with regard to certain common themes for earthbound family members. For example, spirits of children who have taken their lives might feel most comfortable communicating through a medium who has had extensive experience helping parents of such children. Or a spirit intent on communicating about forgiveness may feel most comfortable with a medium who has shared this message with many others.

It's fascinating to me that one week I may do a series of readings that connect with moms in spirit who all have concerns about a family member's physical or emotional health. Then another week, grandmas might come through from spirit to provide advice on how to find passion and happiness. A common theme often seems to arise, and this allows me to become more effective at conveying advice from loved ones in spirit.

As happens with people in the earth plane, the more times I communicate with a specific spirit, the more familiar and trusting our relationship becomes. I have many clients who have had readings for over a decade, sometimes once or twice a year, and each time I feel closer to both them and their loved ones in spirit.

I deeply respect my service to support spirit communication. I also greatly enjoy the limitless sacred wisdom, extensive knowledge, compassionate understanding, and fascinating stories of past and present lives shared from the world of spirit.

MY BUDDY

Messages from the spirit world reminded Maria that her soul purpose was to honor and love herself and forgive the past. She received valuable karmic lessons that set her free from her pain and suffering through the healing of forgiveness.

Maria was raised as an only child in a home with limited resources and with a mom, Ida, who worked two jobs to support her family. Tony, Maria's dad, was challenged with the disease of alcoholism. As much as Maria tried to be playful with her father, he was often cranky with hangovers and unable to receive or respond to her affection because of his guilt. On Maria's eighth birthday, her father left and never returned. Maria often felt tremendous remorse about her father leaving and blamed herself, especially on each of her birthdays.

When Maria was in high school, Ida remarried to Stewart, a factory foreman with a needy desire for attention. Maria fell asleep many nights to the humiliating quarrelling of her mom and stepdad. As soon as she completed high school, she left her unsettling childhood and moved away to college far from home, graduating with a nursing degree.

Maria married a successful businessman, who travelled often. She learned within a short time that he was not emotionally available and was unfaithful on his business trips. Her husband left her, and once again, Maria felt humiliated and abandoned. Soon after Maria's divorce, her mom had a stroke and passed away.

The nurses who worked with Maria encouraged her to contact me for a reading to help her heal from her painful suffering and guilt-ridden past. When she arrived for her reading, she seemed apprehensive and sad. As soon as she sat down, I heard a female spirit with an "I" name who felt like a motherly vibration, and Maria said her mom's name was Ida.

Ida presented evidence in the form of her sudden stroke, her hard work during Maria's childhood, and her divorce.

To Maria's surprise, her mom asked her for forgiveness. Maria's eyes filled with tears as she explained how guilty she felt for leaving her mom and not visiting her much after high school. Ida encouraged Maria to forgive herself. She reminded her of all the good she did to respect herself by getting a college degree and compassionately serving so many ill patients as a nurse.

Ida acknowledged her disappointment that her second husband changed her will so Maria was left with nothing. The heartfelt love of a mother and daughter who were imprisoned by guilt and shame for so many years felt instantly healed. "Please forgive me for my poor choices," Ida communicated from spirit. I explained to Maria that the karma she had with her parents was to help her understand her sense of worth and to experience the powerful freedom of forgiveness.

Tony also visited during Maria's reading. I felt the presence of the father who had abandoned her when she was young. Maria's father identified himself by his alcoholism and his inability to keep a job. Clairvoyantly, I saw him lying on the couch in his white T-shirt and tattered shorts, covered with an orange afghan. Maria validated this with her memory of him. With mercy, Tony communicated that he was learning to forgive himself for abandoning Maria and her mother, and assured her that his sudden departure had nothing to do with her. He acknowledged that February was important to Maria (it was her birthday month) and he said he felt much guilt for abruptly leaving her. "Forgive yourself, my girl, as I learn to forgive myself. You are innocent," Tony communicated.

Once again, Maria was overwhelmed with relief, but she still felt sadness for the years missed with her dad. Finally, Tony handed

Maria a bouquet of vibrant sunflowers as a symbol that he was with her and reminded her to value and love herself. As the sunflower stands tall with a strong beauty, holding its head toward the light, Tony encouraged her to do the same.

The following year, Maria returned for another reading. Both her parents visited during the reading and shared their joy at attending her recent beach wedding. They commented that they loved her cream-colored dress and the sunflowers she carried as her bouquet. Maria confirmed she'd been married five months earlier on a beach in Maui.

Her parents could see so much happiness in her new life, and they communicated they knew a baby was coming. Maria smiled with the glow of a mom as she said she was three months pregnant.

Stewart, Maria's stepfather, visited during this reading as well. He had a great deal of gratitude for the care that Maria gave him at the end of his life, especially as his own children had abandoned him. He provided evidence that he had had Alzheimer's and that his children had taken over his estate. He asked for forgiveness for not being more kind and gracious to Maria and her mom. He explained that as he'd reviewed his life, he'd learned much about the value of self-love and letting go of judgment. "You have found a loving husband because you have learned to forgive and love yourself first," Stewart kindly conveyed to Maria.

Next, I felt the presence of a large black dog with a colorful collar, and I saw the letter "B" on a tag. He was holding a tennis ball in his mouth and showed me he liked to go to a park where there were large oak trees and a big field to play catch. Maria smiled and said her lab Buddy had passed recently and she wondered if he would come to visit for the reading. I felt so much love from Buddy to Maria, and he communicated that she made the right choice by letting him go. He brought my attention to pain in his hips and problems with his kidneys. Maria cried and said Buddy had been suffering with bad arthritis and his kidney and bladder weren't functioning properly. She had taken him to the park almost every day to play fetch and still kept his rainbow collar by the door.

In my mind, I kept seeing bumblebees, too. I asked Maria how Buddy was associated with bees. She grinned and said Buddy habitually chased bees, and Maria would say to her friends that he was as busy as a bee because he never sat still. When Buddy passed, Maria's friends purchased a stuffed little busy bee doll for her, which she keeps near Buddy's urn.

Maria asked if she would ever see her Buddy again, and I explained how pets are important members of the soul family. Significant to Maria, Buddy was teaching her the lessons of unrestricted love and the idea to be present to know joy. He would be sitting, wagging his tail and ready to meet her in spirit, when it was her time to cross.

All three of Maria's parents and Buddy reminded her that they were all together as they continued their spiritual growth, with the understanding of the powerful healing that forgiveness provides each soul. Maria's parents in spirit concluded their communication by letting her know that all three of them would be guardian angels to her new child.

The spirit world often reminds sitters that forgiveness will set them free from the misgivings, doubts, and fears of the past—a most beautiful and encouraging message from our spirit buddies.

A FRIENDLY SMILE

The most shared messages from spirit involve the complications of the heart, the sincere meaning of love, and the application of loving kindness. The essence of our being is love—an authentic and genuine love without expectations, measures, or conditions. Master love and you will know your godlike and blessed self.

For many years, Kathy lived a life with conditional love and challenging relationships. Her father abandoned her and her mom when she was a little girl. Her mom was involved in the theater and wasn't available to help raise her. Her grandma Kathy, her namesake, raised her throughout her childhood until she left for a career in the Navy. After three divorces and many health problems, Kathy phoned me for a reading to try to get clarity on her life purpose and understand her failed relationships.

The first loved one to present for her reading was a grandfather vibration with the name Joe, and in my mind's eye, Joe was on a tractor, plowing a field of wheat. Kathy explained that her grandfather had been a farmer and had grown wheat and corn. Joe saluted Kathy and I saw him in a white T-shirt with a white cap. Laughing, Kathy explained that they made sense to her as both she and Joe had served in the Navy.

Kathy said her grandfather was called Red, but she found out after the reading that his real name was Joe. He communicated that he had passed from lung cancer but had spent the last years of his life isolated from people and connecting with nature. He reminded

Kathy of the time they went for long walks in the forest when she was a child.

Her grandfather suggested Kathy review her relationships to sense the conflicts, conditional love, and lack of self-love she had experienced in them. Kathy was pleased with her grandfather's wisdom and commented that she kept finding herself married to men who demanded conditions throughout her marriages.

Next, Kathy's mom Tina presented herself from spirit to ask her for forgiveness for not being available during her years as a child. Tina showed me a theater and many different costumes she'd worn on stage. Kathy confirmed that her mom had been a traveling stage actress, and throughout her childhood, her mom had been absent. I sensed lung problems connected to Tina's passing, and that she needed her daughter's help with physical challenges at the end of her life. I could smell heavy perfumes and cigarette smoke. As validated by Kathy, her mom had contracted COPD and was a very heavy smoker. When Kathy was stationed overseas for the Navy, she was given a brief time to visit her mom to help her the last two weeks of her life. Kathy felt a sense of guilt for not having had a good relationship with her mom, but Tina reminded her that she had not been available most of her own life to support Kathy. She conveyed forgiveness to Kathy and said now that she was in spirit, she could be more present to provide guidance telepathically.

Tina acknowledged Kathy's recent divorce and advised her not to judge herself too harshly, as Tina had done with many of her own failed relationships. Tina communicated that the soul agreement within their soul family was to trust in love and learn how to love self with no conditions. Many of Kathy's family members and people close to her had succumbed to heart and lung issues of the heart chakra.

As Tina wisely shared, during her life review she realized that she and those she'd shared her life with had felt vulnerable in matters of love. She had had fearful expectations and conditions when loving others. She wanted Kathy to reflect on this same distrust and suspicion in matters of love so Kathy could find authentic love for herself.

Kathy told me that one of her grandmothers, both grandfathers, a brother, and both her parents had passed from either heart or lung problems. She also let me know that the husband she was divorcing had COPD and was in hospice preparing to cross over.

I shared that the physical body is a living autobiography of the emotions, beliefs, thoughts, karma, and feelings that are carried within the energy field around the body. In time, the dysfunctions or disruptions of energy within the aura can manifest as a disease or a physical, emotional, or mental dysfunction within a person. Kathy realized that her respiratory problems must have been due to her inability to love herself unconditionally and her fear of trusting in love.

The following year, Kathy scheduled another phone session, and her parents returned to congratulate her on her move and the progress she'd made—falling in love. Kathy informed me she had just moved across the country to be with the man who'd been her Naval commanding officer three years ago. They agreed to start dating and quickly fell in love. Kathy explained she learned that both Tom (her love) and she had feared loving the other but had always been drawn to each other.

A male spirit then came through by the name of Ray or Roy. He was in a Navy uniform and showed, in my mind, the state of Alaska. Kathy confirmed that Roy was one of her husbands from the Navy, whom she'd met in Alaska. The surprising message from Roy was that he was smiling for Kathy that she had found love and was being brave enough to believe in it. He apologized to Kathy for taking his life and not being emotionally available during their brief marriage. He acknowledged that she tried to save him and love him, but he was unable to share love and had many blocks to emotional and mental intimacy.

Roy showed me an award with stars worn on a dark blue uniform and an image of a smiley face with sunglasses and teeth exposed. Kathy laughed with amazement that, to her surprise, Roy knew about her Navy star award. She explained that they'd both been Naval dentists, and they often sent smiley faces with a mouthful of teeth to each other. Roy also said that anytime she saw the Navy flag, it was a sign to remind her of all the people she assisted in the military and to feel pleased with her service career.

A father vibration mentally appeared to me in a uniform and was applauding with white gloves on. He said the name Richard and indicated he'd been a successful salesman. Kathy confirmed that this was her father. Richard said he was sorry he'd abandoned Kathy when she was a child and that he'd learned in spirit to be more selfless and less selfish. He presented Kathy with a medal of honor for healing through the matters of self-love that she and her soul family had been working through. Of interest, Kathy had in her purse a medal of honor, the only memorabilia from her father.

Tom, Kathy's partner, was sitting in on the phone reading, and a lovely spirit with long curls of gold who had passed from COPD presented herself in a yellow dress. He was pleased that his former wife Joyce showed up for the reading. She thanked him for keeping her home her last days and for painting her bedroom yellow, her favorite color. She asked him for forgiveness for the many years of anger she'd brought into their marriage and recognized the truly loving soul he was. Joyce communicated that she sat with him often in his woodshop and felt the joy he had from making furniture. Tom felt much healing as he harbored guilt for surviving while his wife suffered. Yes, his passion was making furniture, and he was currently making a dining room table for his new love.

Kathy and Tom both said their readings helped them to understand their soul purpose: to trust in love and to accept love of self. As presented in several readings they each had received over the years, they would not have had the will to reconnect with each other, if it hadn't been for the wisdom from spirit. A love of happiness, joy, and contentment was possible, and their loved ones in spirit guided them toward it. They appreciated all the inspiring messages gifted to them from their soul family members and would celebrate their love with all of them in mind.

YOU TAKE IT WITH YOU

The only item you pack—or *can* pack—on your journey to the spirit world is your karma. Some of us have more "luggage" than others. Simply stated, only karma goes with you to spirit! Karma is the product of the law of cause and effect, the universal principle that every word, thought, or action results in an equal and precise reaction. In other words, you get back what you put out, or you reap what you sow. You take that harvest (karma) with you wherever you go, even into spirit. To be free of negative karma, you must resolve it with love.

I'm frequently asked by sitters if their loved ones approve of what was done with their belongings. To the surprise of many, loved ones in spirit are much more concerned with the intentions and kindness associated with the distribution of their possessions than the belongings themselves.

The most troubling messages I convey in readings have to do with the discord a family member creates with the unjust distribution of their loved one's belongings. Family members have demonstrated just plain selfishness in the unjust distribution of the deceased's possessions or in disregarding their loved one's wishes.

Your loved ones in spirit will remind family members that every choice and the intention of the choice create karma, positive or negative. Allow me to share two readings in which loved ones in spirit were greatly disappointed in the family conflicts that occurred when one or a few family members challenged the rest of the family.

Sadly, it happens much too often, even when someone leaves a formal will.

GRACE AND HER BROTHERS

Grace owned her own accounting business in Washington, DC and was highly successful. When she learned that her father had developed Lou Gehrig's disease, she closed her business to move back to Chicago to help her parents. Her father Michael was most grateful that Grace came home but encouraged her to keep her business running. The final year of Michael's life was most challenging because Grace's mom Marie was diagnosed with Alzheimer's disease. Grace had two brothers and asked if they could return home to help her care for both parents, but her brothers replied they were too busy with their own families and careers.

After six years as a devoted caretaker, Grace buried both parents and was in the process of taking care of their estate. She was distraught to learn that while her mother was suffering with dementia, her brothers had come home one weekend to "watch" her, taken her to their longtime family attorney, and seen to it the will was changed. Grace was completely written out of the will. Why would her mom do this to her? Grace was dismayed.

She scheduled the first of several readings with me to try to understand the circumstances of her parents' estate and get some clarity from her parents in spirit. Michael presented himself as a successful doctor and showed me that he had received many awards, had given international lectures, and was well known in the field of healing children. Grace validated that her father had been chief of pediatric medicine, had lectured all over the world, and had published in many medical journals.

Michael shared how much he appreciated Grace's tremendous responsibility in taking care of her mother and him, and he encouraged her to thrive in her accounting business. He also impressed upon me his displeasure with his sons for changing matters of his estate. I could hear Grace begin to cry on the phone. He showed me an image of an apple pie (which Grace confirmed was his favorite dessert), and the intention was for the pie to be split equally three ways, but I saw it cut in half. She explained that her brothers had written her out of the will that their father had crafted years before his passing.

Next, I felt the presence of a mother vibration with a name beginning with "M" come through, and she showed me that she had memory issues before she passed. I saw a beautiful formal garden with a wide variety of colored roses and a huge home with marble floors and high ceilings. Grace identified this as her mother, Marie, and explained that she had suffered with Alzheimer's, had been exceedingly wealthy, and had spent most of her time with the garden society. Marie had won many awards for her roses and her extraordinary rose garden.

Grace asked her mom why she would agree to write her out of her father's will. Marie had no memory of agreeing to this and said she was doing all she could to try to telepathically encourage Grace's brothers to share the estate. Marie communicated that she wanted peace with her children, and that although she had often shown favor to her sons, she loved Grace dearly.

Grace's parents encouraged her to contest the will and even provided the name Robert, one of Michael's longtime business attorneys. They asked Grace to make every effort to not let the situation with her brothers cause her distress and anxiety. Leave it in the hands of the professionals and know that you will receive a portion of the pie, but it will take time, they communicated.

For eight years, Grace had annual readings, and she grew weary to the point of developing heart problems because of the hate she had for her brothers. She asked for updates at each reading, especially from her father, but he was more concerned with Grace's mental state and physical health. In time, she was granted a small portion of the estate, a home that she wanted more than anything. Her loved ones in spirit communicated over and over their greatest concern was for her well-being and the progression of her soul. Let go of your fears and ruthless thoughts about your brothers, she was told continually throughout her readings.

Grace finally found contentment in her life, and although she no longer associated with her brothers, she learned to forgive them and her mom and focus on having a family of her own.

FIVE SIBLINGS

Another example demonstrating selfish cruelty between siblings emerged in a series of individual in-person and phone readings with five siblings over the course of several years. I find myself in an uncomfortable situation when quarreling siblings ask for readings, often not knowing the others had readings also. The same family members from the spirit world came through and regularly explained how conflict is an ideal occasion to surrender, forgive, and release karma to heal the soul. Spirit was not taking sides but consistently providing advice to find inner peace and preserve family connections.

Maryanne scheduled a reading to communicate with her father in spirit about her great concerns for her mother. I felt the presence of a strong male spirit, and in my mind's eye, he showed me a short, bald male figure, sitting behind a desk with shelves of matching books and a desk full of contracts. I also saw For Sale signs, which helped me understand that this spirit was successful in the profession of real estate, and he had an association with law. Maryanne confirmed that her father, William, had been a successful real estate attorney in LA, and he'd often spent time in his office.

William showed me concerns over a family issue and a contract. He presented me the number 5, and Maryanne said there were five children in the family. Using my clairaudient intuition, I could hear William say that, in his will, he'd left everything to his wife, and then when his wife passed, all children were to receive an equal portion. William showed me the letter "A" and associated this with his attorney, who handled all of his matters while he was still in the earth plane. Maryanne verified the name Allan, and she said he had been her father's much trusted attorney for over forty years.

I saw conflict with three against three in matters of changing the will. Maryanne commented that two of her sisters and her mother were trying to challenge the will. The two oldest sisters, Joanne and Jean, had moved in to care for their mother and insisted that they get the house, and the stocks and bonds could be equally split between all five siblings.

Powerfully, I felt the presence of a grandfather spirit connected to the mother's side of the family, and I heard the name George. George was concerned about the health and well-being of his daughter Julia (Maryanne's mother). The family conflict was causing great emotional strain on Julia, and her cancer was spreading from her respiratory system to her digestive system. Maryanne confirmed this, and she was miserable because her older sisters Joanne and Jean were preventing their mom from having any contact with other family members.

Grandpa George was also not pleased that two of his granddaughters would try to undo what his daughter and son-in-law worked hard to build for the family. He asked Maryanne to continue to have her other siblings and their children send cards and letters to Julia, even though she might not ever receive them. The intention of sending healing, love, and kindness to their mother Julia was the most important thing they could do.

Two of Maryanne's brothers, Gus and Joe, came together to see me for a reading, telling me their sister Maryanne had had a recent phone reading. Their messages from their father and maternal grandfather in spirit were consistent with Maryanne's. The messages urged the brothers to try to communicate with their mother, as her illness had worsened. Gus and Joe confirmed their mom was in hospice care and they knew she had a limited time left here.

Helen, a high-energy grandmotherly spirit, got my attention. In my mind, she showed me her quilts, her sewing basket, and shears. She was sitting in her favorite wooden rocker (as validated by her grandsons) and was singing her favorite church hymns, such as

"Amazing Grace" and "How Great Thou Art." Gus smiled and said his Grandma Helen had been well known for her quilts and her religion. She surprised her grandsons by communicating that she knew they had surprised their mom at the hospital after hours one night recently. Grandma Helen said the visit made their mom feel so much better.

Even though the brothers still had no communication with Joanne and Jean, Grandma Helen encouraged her grandsons to let go of their anger and reflect on all that was given to them. She assured them their father and grandparents in spirit loved them dearly. She acknowledged that they were both loving fathers and little league coaches. Their intentions were just and true, she affirmed, and she was very proud of them.

Joe asked his grandma if they would win this family fight. Sensibly, Grandma Helen assured them that the finest outcome would regard the healing of their souls as a soul family. She reminded them that results in the earth plane are inconsequential compared to the consequences concerning their souls. Before leaving the reading, Grandma Helen blessed her grandsons and said to always be loving and kind to others, for it will bring you a sense of grateful contentment.

Each family member in such a situation will experience grief in a unique way. Sometimes, individuals who gravitate toward fear will tend to want their loved one's belongings all for themselves, falsely believing this will bring them closer to their loved one. The powerless tend to believe that the more they have, the better they will feel, even at the expense of taking from other family members. In truth, love cannot be bought or fulfilled with objects.

Even if much effort goes into the thoughtful planning of a loved one's estate, the person's wishes aren't always followed. Once people leave the physical plane to enter spirit, they are no longer attached to their property or belongings, but they remain attached to those they love.

The karma you create by disrespecting others you will need to resolve in your future. The karma you create by being loving and kind is your most valuable asset and one you will have forever.

THERE ARE NO ACCIDENTS

The occurrences in a specific soul's life are highly integrated into all universal incidences simultaneously, with sacred perfection and divine timing. What may be considered a mishap can be a moment of enlightenment; it's all a matter of perspective. There are no random coincidences or accidents. Ever.

One afternoon, as I reflected on my next client, Rose, I felt tremendous fear, grief, and a sense of blame over a recent loss. It all felt as if it related to a younger male. The colors pink, green, and yellow came into my mind, which allowed me to intuit that Rose was a highly nurturing person; she was in service to others, especially within her family; and she was working on being more confident and empowered.

Rose came to her reading with a younger female and asked if it was all right for her to sit in. I agreed. As soon as Rose sat down, I felt the presence of a father vibration, and he telepathically showed me fruit trees and bushel baskets filled with lemons and oranges. He was a short man with dark features, wearing gloves. I could intuitively hear him say, with a thick Spanish accent, that he had had stomach cancer. With a delightful smile, Rose said this must be her father from Mexico. He had owned a farm with fruit trees in California.

Although she was pleased with her father's visit, she said she urgently wanted to communicate with someone else. I told Rose that when I do a spirit reading, I politely acknowledge whoever comes through and accept the sequence in which they present themselves.

As I often remind sitters, first and foremost, I am in service to spirit but will do my best to provide the desired connections. However, the deceased must also trust the medium and feel comfortable communicating through the mediumship process.

I asked Rose to allow her father to complete his message, and later in the reading, we could ask for other spirits. Rose's father said he appreciated all she had done to help and accommodate all her family's needs when they migrated to California, and he was proud that she worked in the medical field. Rose confirmed she had arranged for her parents to move to California, and she had studied to become an assistant nurse.

Rose's father communicated that with him in spirit was a younger male, in his early twenties, whom he was meeting for the first time. This younger male appeared in my mind's eye wearing a blue baseball hat. He had dark hair, was tall, and had dimples when he smiled. He told me he enjoyed playing baseball, and I could hear him say "third base."

Rose cried with relief, knowing her dad was with her son and that his consciousness was still alive. Rose said she felt her son was present, and sensing a loved one's presence from the spirit world is the ultimate gift of a reading.

I couldn't hear his name and asked Rose to provide it so I could try to better link to her son. She said his name was Brad and confirmed that his passion had been baseball and he'd played third base. Brad next showed me a garage filled with cars with their hoods up, and he had a wrench in his hand. Rose said that her son had been a mechanic and had belonged to a car club.

Brad communicated that he was sorry he left without saying goodbye, and he showed me that he instantly left his body when a van-like vehicle hit his black car on a major highway. Rose confirmed that her son had been in an accident with a small bus (like a van) on a major freeway. She was relieved to know he'd left his body quickly and hadn't suffered.

Rose said she would believe more strongly if I would say a code word she asked Brad to convey before the reading. As I explain to sitters, I told her I provide insights communicated to me, and I had received no specific code word. I believe our loved ones in spirit don't like to be tested and mediumship requires a level of trust and faith.

I asked Brad if he wanted to share any more messages with his mom, and I telepathically heard him say he would like to speak to the other lady with his mom.

Danika had come to the reading with Rose, and she said she was open to receive his messages. Brad conveyed that he'd enjoyed their trip to San Diego and he was pleased she'd decided to return to college. Danika told me she was Brad's fiancée, and the last trip they'd taken together was to San Diego. She also confirmed she'd just begun classes in business administration at a local community college.

I told Danika I saw a blue glass box and Brad sent a message that it was linked to him. In tears, Rose and Danika held each other and explained that Brad's ashes were in that glass box.

As the reading progressed, Brad felt more comfortable trusting me to communicate with his mom and fiancée. He wanted his mom to know that her sister Eva was with him. Eva presented evidence as Rose's older sister by communicating a vision of a lovely garden of wild flowers. Also, I could smell cigarette smoke, and I heard her say that her smoking contributed to her death from lung disease. Rose confirmed that Eva was her sister and she had died of lung cancer. I then saw the image of sunflowers and lavender, and Eva communicated to share this with her sister Rose. To Rose's amazement, she recalled that those were her sister's favorite flowers to grow.

Before leaving the reading, Eva said her soul had the inner knowing to leave for the spirit world just weeks before Brad's accident so she could help orient him to the other side in appreciation for Rose's care for her during her long illness. Spirits know just before someone will be passing so they are available to help them cross over into the spirit world. Once Eva was in spirit, she would have had this realization that Brad would soon be joining her. Her soul had orchestrated the perfect timing for her own passing.

With cleansing tears and a hoarse voice, Rose acknowledged that she'd been the main caregiver for her sister, who had, in fact, passed several weeks before her son. Eva thanked her sister for allowing her to leave her physical body. She said many family members wanted her to stay, but once Rose let her go by giving her permission to pass on, she was able to transition to the spirit world with peace and grace.

Rose verified that Eva's mom, siblings, and children didn't want her to go. Eva suffered for many months, and Rose prayed that her sister would be released from her pain. It was the right time to let her go, and Eva thanked Rose for being understanding and kindhearted.

Each soul has the ultimate knowing of when is the best time to leave the physical body. Death can be delayed, though, if family members aren't consciously, or subconsciously, willing to let the person go, which can result in more pain and suffering for the individual. Universal timing is always divine and should be trusted. There's usually a significant lesson to be learned about faith and respect in these situations.

Within my mind, I heard Brad say, "There are no accidents in life." Everything is divinely organized and lovingly planned, and Rose was at peace knowing Brad's aunt and grandfather were with him in spirit. Brad communicated that although he had planned to start his own business one day, his soul had important things to achieve and to heal that were best accomplished in the spiritual realm. The earth plane is a more substantial learning plane for certain types of lessons associated with cause and effect, relationships, and the use of the mind because of the colorful and vibrant emotions associated with living here. However, sometimes a soul can gain a greater perspective and understanding of its own divinity by remembering this truth in the higher plane of spirit. Every soul is all-knowing, but most forget the truth when incarnating into the denser vibrations of the earth plane to learn other lessons.

Brad also communicated that he knew both of these loving souls (Rose and Danica) had a fresh perspective on their lives and more urgency to accomplish things they were passionate about. They nodded, through tears, and said they had tried activities they'd never tried before and visited places they'd never been to before. Brad's passing had brought them to a greater level of appreciation and gratitude for the many blessings in their lives.

Danika and Rose asked Brad if they had done the right thing to let him go, as they felt guilty for signing papers to have him taken off life support. Within my heart, I felt a warm feeling and told the ladies Brad said it was very brave of them to allow him to leave, and that it had helped to reinforce their faith. Very clearly, I could hear Brad say that to allow a loved one to go is a wonderfully compassionate act when the person is trapped inside a nonfunctioning body. Providing freedom from a diseased or injured body is a precious and selfless act of unconditional love. Tears filled all our eyes as I shared this tender message from Brad.

Brad brought through a good friend of his with a "D" name, who had passed from a head injury while playing high school football. Rose said yes, this was David, and that she was a good friend of David's mother Judy. David communicated that he wanted Rose to let his mom know that he sat next to her in church, where she lit candles and prayed for him. He was also proud that his mom had started a scholarship for athletes instead of trying to find someone to sue and blame for his passing.

Together, Brad and David shared a momentous and healing message that a soul never leaves the body unless it's time to go. The timing of a person's passing is determined by the free will of each individual. The scheduling of birth into the physical plane and the timing of rebirth into the spiritual plane is perfectly and sacredly divine and is significant to the karmic lessons of everyone associated with that particular soul.

I could feel a calming sense of peace come over the ladies with these messages from their loved ones. Danika asked what Brad was doing on the other side. Brad conveyed that he was reflecting on the many choices he'd made in his life on earth and the influence of his choices on the quality of his life and the lives of those he loved.

Many spirits refer to a life reflection, or life review, after passing into spirit. Each soul has the revered learning opportunity to revisit and feel the consequences of his or her life choices. Imagine how helpful it is to reflect *with no judgment* on specific choices that caused fear, anger, sorrow, or blame, while also considering other decisions that created peace, love, and contentment. Brad wisely ended his communication during the reading by reminding his mom and Danika that a great gift of life is having the freedom to make choices, but wisdom comes from understanding the consequences of each choice.

And so it is.

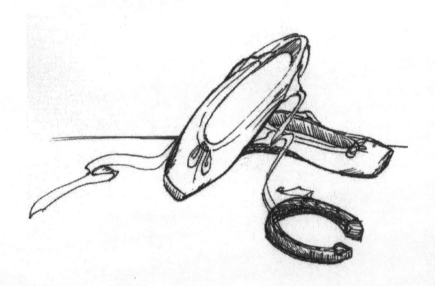

BOTH SIDES NOW

A significant concept I've learned about spirit communication is that our loved ones in spirit are more in control of the mechanism of communication than those of us in the physical plane. As mentioned previously, spirits must feel comfort and trust with the particular medium to be open to communicate. We can ask for specific spirits to present during a reading, but they have free will whether to communicate or not, just as we do.

The more familiar and comfortable the spirit is with the medium, the easier the process of communication will be. Just as you get acquainted with a friend in the physical plane, spirits get to know the medium and their communication becomes stronger and more effective over time. Allow me to present two lovely spirits who took me by surprise and astonished me.

Within a short period of time, during different phone readings, two spirits communicated whom I'd provided readings for while they were in the earth plane. Both spirits mentally conveyed to me that I had connected them with loved ones on the other side, and they had now happily met them in spirit. Often, when spirits are helping me to understand a concept, they present it at least several times so I "get" it and can acknowledge it, too. Wow! Communicating with spirits I had read for when they were here on earth was so amazing—a kind of second generation of spirit communication!

Within the same week, on a Monday and Wednesday, I had two separate telephone readings scheduled with clients from Hawaii and

Florida, respectively. Unknown to me, these two clients were sisters, and they both employed me to connect with the same sister, who had recently passed away from lung cancer.

ELIZABETH AND HER SISTERS

Elizabeth presented herself from the spiritual realm as soon as I began to speak to Susan during her phone reading. Susan confirmed evidence that Elizabeth was a sister connection and that she had suffered with lung cancer for several years. I felt heaviness in breathing, and Elizabeth helped me understand she had needed a constant supply of oxygen, and that one lung had to be removed. This loving spirit wanted to tell her three male "J"s she was all right, and that she was a guardian to her three grandchildren. I could hear Susan crying on the other end of the line as she explained that Elizabeth had had a rough time breathing, and she loved most of all her three grandbabies. I asked Susan if Elizabeth had three sons whose names started with J, and she explained that she had two sons and a husband who were all "J"s.

Then the remarkable happened, as I listened to the spirit of Elizabeth communicate that I had done readings for her in the past, for over ten years, and that she was from Chicago. Immediately I recalled her last few readings and remembered she often had difficulty breathing during our conversations. Elizabeth mentally communicated that just before she passed, she had provided my contact information to Susan so she could understand the comfort Elizabeth had received when she had had her readings connecting with her parents. Susan was simply in awe and said that her reason to phone for a reading was to see if her sister would come through, and if I would know her.

Next, I heard the name Margaret, and I saw in my mind a tall lady with long black hair in a light blue dress and apron, standing in front of a kitchen sink. Susan confirmed that this was her mother. Her mother wanted to let Susan know the whole family had been there to meet Elizabeth, and that she was pleased Susan had visited Elizabeth and stayed with her the last several weeks of her life. After providing Susan with insights about her career and health, her mom and sister assured Susan they would always be with her, especially when she was playing classical music on the piano. Susan thanked me and said she had her mom's piano and often thought of her family while playing Brahms and Chopin.

Two days later, I phoned Krissy for her reading and she told me she was very nervous because she'd never had a reading before. She explained that the main purpose of her reading was to communicate with loved ones. Right away I saw in my mind's eye a tall fireman, and I heard the name John. He felt like a playful and funny spirit, and he showed me his golf clubs, horseshoes, and homemade brick barbeque pit. Krissy was astonished that her father presented such specific evidence, and she was so pleased to welcome him. She explained that they both loved to golf together, and for many family events, her dad loved to cook burgers and dogs on his homemade grill. John wanted Krissy to know he was with a younger lady, who had passed with cancer in the chest. In my mind, I heard him say daughter, that she had been seriously ill for years, and she was now finding comfort out of her physical body.

The female spirit presented herself and said she had recently passed and was pleased that Krissy organized a beautiful service. She loved the music Krissy had played, especially "Wind Beneath My Wings." Also, she communicated that her mom Margaret was with her, and she enjoyed connecting with her family in spirit.

She encouraged Krissy to watch out for her two sons. I heard the names Jake and Josh and that she was with the one in the military uniform overseas. Krissy was stunned that her sister confirmed her two sons by name and that she was watching over Josh, who was in the Middle East, because the family worried about him. Krissy lived away from her sister and hadn't been able to see her much over the last decade, so she was happy her sister liked the funeral mass she had organized.

Last, Krissy's sister conveyed to me mentally that I had done readings for her for many years, and she was so pleased to speak with me again. With a sense of peace, Krissy said I had spoken to her sister Susan earlier in the week, and that her sister Elizabeth had had readings with me for ten years. Susan and Krissy had both promised their sister Elizabeth that they would phone me to connect with her once she was settled in spirit.

LULU AND HER DAUGHTERS

Just a few weeks after these two readings, three nervous and very skeptical sisters came to visit me for a reading. As they sat in my office, the oldest sister explained that as they were going through their mom's belongings, they'd found a notebook with notes from four readings and my name and address. They never knew their mom had been open to speak to a medium, and they felt by finding her notebook that she was encouraging them from spirit to speak to me.

Immediately, I heard the name Louis or Lu, and all three sisters smiled, saying their mom's nickname was Lulu. Lulu had on a pink bathrobe and had curlers in her hair. In my mind, I heard a raspy voice and saw her smoking a cigarette. She showed me she had loved gambling and playing the slots at the casino. The month of April was important to Lulu and she said to tell Sam hello.

With joyful tears, the youngest daughter validated that her mom loved to play the slots, and she and her sisters had bought her a pink bathrobe when she was diagnosed with breast cancer. She also confirmed that her mom's birthday was in April and that Sam was her boyfriend.

Lulu wanted her daughters to know that when they saw heart shapes and pink flowers, it was a sign she was present. The girls were comforted by that idea as they had arranged to have all pink roses at her funeral, and they each had a heart pendant from Lulu as a gift for their last Christmas together.

After providing relationship and career guidance to each of her daughters, I could hear Lulu say to me that she had had several readings with me, and she had hoped her daughters would find her notes. The eldest daughter spoke and said they were highly skeptical about coming to see me because they hadn't had a pleasing experience with another reader. She confirmed that Lulu had seen me several times over the years, and again, I was absolutely astonished that I was communicating with yet another spirit I had read for in the physical plane.

Clairvoyantly, I saw Lulu dancing as a ballerina, and I could hear classical piano music playing. She said her passion was to dance, and I could see Paris and London on a map. The daughters confirmed that their mom had been a professional ballet dancer and had spent most of her career in Paris, London, and New York. Lulu communicated that she loved to play the piano and teach dance in her later years, to which her daughters nodded yes.

I felt the presence of a father from spirit and, in my mind, I saw him in a brown tweed jacket and khakis, and he was sitting at a desk in front of shelves of books. I saw a globe, a world map, and charts with historic timelines in an office, and this man had a bag lunch. The sisters all smiled because their dad, Stan, loved to bring his lunch to work at a local university, where he taught history.

Lulu told me to tell her girls that I was correct in communicating from her husband Phil that he would be there to help her cross over when she passed. Phil conveyed that he still had his dry humor, and while in the earth plane, he had enjoyed gardening at the lake. All three sisters nodded in unison. In closing, Lulu said they loved reminiscing about their vacations at the mountain lake when all three girls were little.

It brings great joy to my heart when I know clients can feel their connection to their loved ones. I was most astounded and overjoyed that I had read for both Elizabeth and Lulu when they were in the body, and that I was able to provide comfort and inspiration to their families still here in the earth plane.

Even after providing spiritual readings for over twenty-five years, I'm still astonished at how our loved ones in spirit send their loving kindness and gracious encouragement to lend a hand on our journey of enlightenment. Carl Sagan said, "Somewhere, something incredible is waiting to be known." As a medium, I continually discover fresh perspectives and experience novel insights when communicating with spirit.

Judy Collins sang, "I've looked at life from both sides now." It heartens me to understand how Elizabeth and Lulu could fully embrace awareness from both the physical and spiritual planes through the remarkable process of mediumship.

PART 5

THE MESSAGE

MEANINGS OF MESSAGES, SIGNS, AND SYMBOLS

*"Language, in its origin and essence, is simply a system
of signs and symbols that denote real occurrences or
their echo in the human soul."* ~ Carl Jung

The most encouraging and astonishing messages from our loved ones in spirit require the active participation of spirit, the sitter, and of course, the medium. Optimal spirit communication occurs when the spirit, the sitter, and the medium are focused, present, and completely open. When this synergy exists, the message is more likely to be strong, clearly received, and understood.

Initially, I encourage spirits to present evidence of who they are. This could be their name or initials, an important month or date(s), common duties or hobbies, accomplishments, religious or political beliefs, health issues, their career, or their connection to the sitter. This evidence isn't a means for me to prove my abilities; rather, such detail helps to ensure that I know, and the sitter knows, who is coming through. Spirits usually astutely use evidence that's both literal and symbolic, and more significantly, details that the sitter would recognize as associated with that person or the sitter.

Many times, sitters don't know a spirit, and I encourage them to note the information and validate it after the reading with another family member. I enjoy hearing later from sitters who share details about an ancestor they didn't know about during the reading. It confirms I wasn't reading their mind or heart, but truly connecting with a spirit who was somehow associated with the sitter.

Once the evidence is presented, the most important aspect of the reading happens. Loved ones in spirit enjoy the unique opportunity to ask for forgiveness, offer their appreciation, or clarify their reason for a certain life event. They might encourage the sitter's growth and development as a soul or offer family and relationship advice, to name a few possibilities. Spirits don't make choices or decisions for you as they won't violate the law of free will. They will help you to understand the consequences of your choices, but the choice is always yours.

No message is to be regarded as simple or meaningless. Your loved ones in spirit are creative and wise in their ability to share messages that will touch your heart and inspire your mind. The enjoyment for me, as the receiver of the heartfelt messages, is to help you comprehend what your loved ones are expressing.

LITERAL AND SYMBOLIC MEANING

Usually, specific literal evidence is presented, for example, grandma hand drying the dishes and sweeping the kitchen, or dad sitting in his favorite leather chair reading a history book. These activities and settings help you identify specific loved ones. The greater meaning of a message is symbolic. Perhaps grandma in the kitchen sweeping is communicating a concern about how to clean up family challenges, or dad is asking you to review your history as symbolized by the history books.

A great mystical and magical viewpoint is presented in each and every aspect of a reading. As Albert Einstein wisely said, "The most beautiful thing we can experience is the mysterious; it is the source of all true art and science." You're more likely to comprehend the profound but subtle meanings of your loved ones' mysterious messages after a time of contemplation. A message that's not understood or is misunderstood probably hasn't been completely interpreted. I encourage you to actively process the messages and feel their meaning over time.

The most important meaning of any message received will only be completely understood within the heart. Sit with your messages in a tranquil place and sense their significance. Feel the energy of the message. Antoine de Saint-Exupéry presents this concept well in his book *The Little Prince,* in which he states, "One sees clearly with the heart. Anything essential is invisible to the eyes."

To me, the most fascinating aspect of spirit communication is the level of genius and pure creativity presented in the messages. The artistic quality and creativity used to present specific heartfelt messages and remarkable signs demonstrate the great originality that goes into the loving messages gifted from spirit.

Symbols specific to the spirit and unique to the sitter are masterfully presented to enhance the feeling and healing potential of the message. Spirits have a unique code of communication based on their habits, hobbies, beliefs, life trials, and personality while they were in the physical body. Also, the message is crafted to accommodate the awareness level of the sitter as well as the sitter's passions, attitudes, and perceptions. For example, I am passionate and fondly aware of nature, so spirit utilizes signs from nature to communicate with me. A butterfly or hummingbird, the breeze blowing, a colorful flower in my path, or an animal totem may be presented at the perfect moment to encourage my understanding of a particular choice or decision.

Remember that your loved ones in spirit are always communicating with you—through the songs on the radio, the people in your day-to-day life, and your daily circumstances and situations. Be open, be still, reflect, and connect. Loving messages are all around you. Spirit is resourceful and inventive at using many means to say hello, I love you, or you're okay.

Following are examples of readings in which loved ones in spirit demonstrate how creative they are at presenting messages with clever literal meanings as well as ingenious symbolism. Messages have many layers of meaning, and it's vitally important to comprehend and appreciate their value and significance to your soul.

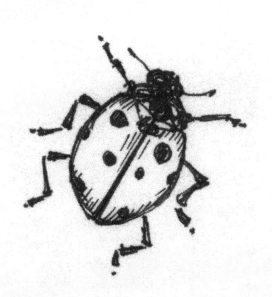

LADYBUG HUGS

Your loved ones in spirit communicate on a continuous basis to encourage and intuitively assist you with both small and big life choices. They take pleasure in letting you know they are present to celebrate your life achievements and encourage and support you in challenging hardships. It's valuable to recognize specific signs that loved ones in spirit provide to you so you can feel and know their presence.

As a medium, I can present similar signs from spirit, but their meaning is specific to the individual sitter. Just as road signs show a driver which direction and how fast to drive, a sign from spirit can remind you of a specific choice or path that may benefit you on your road trip through life.

Many times when I present a sign during a reading, the sitter can relate to it; but sometimes spirits want a loved one to watch for a particular sign. This is a creative, meaningful, and fun way for your loved ones in spirit to let you know they are with you. I often find the magnificence of nature provides the ideal symbolic and literal signs to ensure we know our connections are eternal and sacred. There are often literal meanings to a sign, but the ingenious symbolism is the scrumptious delight of the reading. Allow me to demonstrate the significance of a ladybug from two very different readings.

KERI

Keri was sad that her Grandma Lucy had passed before Keri was able to complete her college education, get married, and become a mom. For her high school graduation gift, her mother Sandy purchased an in-person reading.

As I sat with Keri, I immediately felt the presence of two grandmothers who wanted to communicate with an exceedingly nervous Keri. It's common to be nervous for a reading, so I told Keri to take a big breath and open her heart so she could feel the presence of the loved ones who would visit during the reading.

The first grandma communicated that she was a large lady who had extreme circulatory problems and kidney disease. She hadn't known Keri in the physical but had been a guardian to her for her entire life. This grandma showed me her connection to Keri's father, how she loved to cook tomato sauce, enjoyed playing the piano, and made her own wine. Keri's father often spoke of his mom, so Keri knew most of these things, but she would have to check with her dad about the piano. Grandma confirmed that Keri had just graduated and was going away to college to study business.

A second grandma came through connected to Keri's mom. Clairvoyantly, I could see that this grandma had an "L" on her shirt and was a short lady with bright red hair. She was dressed very nicely, and she told me to tell Keri she appreciated her keeping the dolls. Keri was quite surprised that the little details presented made her feel connected again to her Grandma Lucy. No matter what, Keri said, she would never part with her dolls, especially because one of them had the same red hair color as Grandma's.

Next, I saw a tennis racquet and golf clubs, and Grandma Lucy and Keri both laughed because Grandma preferred those sports over cooking and cleaning. Grandma had tennis shoes on and encouraged me to communicate that she was always on the go. It was special for Keri to know that her grandma was at her high school graduation in spirit and that Grandma loved how Keri sang at the ceremony. Grandma said she loved Keri and was proud of all she had accomplished, and she looked forward to her success in business school.

Sign of Grandma's Presence

To make sure she knew when Grandma Lucy was with her, Keri requested I ask for a sign. My imagination kept displaying lovely ladybugs. I then psychically heard Grandma tell me to share with Keri she would know Grandma was present when a ladybug visits. At the time of the reading, this didn't make sense to Keri, but as she left, she promised she would be on the lookout for ladybugs.

Several years passed and Keri came to visit me again. She was astonished how her Grandma had shown her presence with ladybugs. On the morning that Keri left for college, a windy thunderstorm began as she sadly said goodbye to her family. She explained to me that tears filled her eyes and it was hard to see because of the rain, too. As she pulled out of the driveway, a ladybug landed on her hand. She felt great joy to know she was not alone. Then she told me that the following Christmas at the holiday dinner, her mom and she were saying how they missed the presence of Grandma Lucy. In the frozen winter, at the dinner table, a ladybug landed on Keri's plate of turkey and dressing.

The most recent ladybug from Grandma was the most significant to Keri, though. With tears of joy, Keri explained she'd gotten married last month. As her parents were getting ready to escort her down the aisle, a ladybug crawled onto her hand from her bouquet of cream roses, Grandma's favorite flower, affirming that Grandma Lucy was present for her special day.

MELISSA

Melissa's experience offers a second example of a spirit using the sign of a ladybug. Melissa came to a reading to find comfort for her overwhelming grief. Sitting with her, I smelled the tantalizing odor of grilling hot dogs and saw a gas grill in a fenced-in backyard.

I detected a gentleman with blue jeans, a sleeveless shirt, and a red baseball cap grilling and singing country western tunes. Tears flowed down Melissa's cheeks as she recognized this as her husband Ronnie because he loved to cook out in their yard, and he often sang Johnny Cash and Merle Haggard songs. Ronnie then showed me a red pickup truck and said it was okay to give it away. To Melissa's relief, she explained that she'd given Ronnie's truck away to a good friend because it pained her to see it every day.

In my mind, I saw a mountain lake and heard Ronnie say he'd loved being back home. He communicated that he'd enjoyed fishing and hunting in the mountains and appreciated the outdoor memorial service Melinda had organized for him. I then heard the song "Stairway to Heaven," and Melinda excitedly explained that they'd played that song at his service by the lake.

Sign of a Good Choice

With all the changes going on in Melinda's life, she wanted to know if Ronnie could send her a sign to show her she was making the right choices. Ronnie showed me ladybugs and Melinda began to cry. She explained that the previous weekend, she had visited the site where she'd buried his ashes. She wasn't sure it was the right place but knew he loved to sit on tree stumps deep in the woods near the lake where he had fished and hunted. On that weekend when she went to visit the grave, the tree stump had been covered with thousands of ladybugs. She knew it must have been a sign, and now the message from her reading validated it.

Ronnie communicated that he would send her a visual in her mind, an image using technology or the real thing, to give her confidence when she was making tough decisions. He shared that he supported her with all her choices but encouraged her to follow her heart. He also communicated to Melinda that the only options to choose to improve the quality of her life were choices of kindheartedness. "I love you with all my heart," he told Melinda.

Ronnie also affirmed that in the world of spirit there was only peace and love.

Each sign is specific to the receiver of the message. For Keri, the ladybug meant the spirit of her Grandma Lucy was present, and for Melinda, the ladybug was confirmation that her decisions were in the loving significance of her soul. Nature has a wonderfully inspiring way to help loved ones in spirit share their messages by offering the magic of a ladybug hug.

PENNY LOAFERS

Marylyn loves her shoes! Her late husband Joe often teased her about how every closet in their home was overflowing with her shoes. Every Easter, New Year's Eve, and anniversary Marylyn enjoyed shopping for new shoes to celebrate her life. Joe used to keep an old mason jar on his dresser of coins he'd saved, and each Christmas he'd give them to Marylyn for her shoe fund.

Grief overcame Marylyn and she reluctantly decided to try a mediumship reading to see if she could hear from Joe and receive a sign of his presence. Initially, Marylyn's father-in-law Joe Sr. appeared from spirit during the reading. He showed himself sitting behind a desk with ledgers and a calculator. He said he was good with numbers and Marylyn confirmed he was an accountant and worked from a desk in his home. Joe Sr. thanked her for taking good care of his son during his difficult time with pancreatic cancer. He communicated that Joe Jr. and he were fishing and reviewing their lives. He communicated that the spirit world is a very lovely place and there's so much loving kindness there.

Next, I felt the presence of a fatherly vibration with the same name sitting at a desk with many books. The books were associated with Edgar Cayce, the afterlife, and higher consciousness. With an excited reply, Marylyn let me know that she had wanted to hear from her dad for many years but had been unable to connect with him in spirit. Her father introduced her to Edgar Cayce books and books on spirituality—especially higher consciousness.

Marylyn had been connecting with loved ones in her meditation for many years and had wondered why her father hadn't come through. Her father presented himself with a smile, sitting in an Adirondack chair in the front yard, observing a family of deer. As validated by Marylyn, her father often sat in that type of chair, and she thought of her father when she saw deer. Marylyn's dad shared the message that the deer were symbolic for the admiration he had for her meditation practice and her ability to sit in silence and understand the gentleness of her heart. He told her that in the spiritual realm, there was much stillness and tranquility.

Marylyn's paternal grandfather then mentally appeared, with a large axe, shovel, and flashlight. She laughed, saying grandpa was a coal miner in England, and he often communicated with her during meditation. Grandfather presented his flashlight on his helmet, near his third eye, to symbolically let Marylyn know he was helping her to connect with her intuition. He also complemented Marylyn on her journaling after meditation, and he encouraged her to complete a book she was writing. Grandfather communicated that Marylyn was writing about her illness and her preparation for her passing. He told Marylyn her book would be helpful to the healing of many other souls, and he encouraged her to finish the book and put her heartfelt feelings and soul wisdom into her writings. Unknown to me, Marylyn had stage four leukemia and was in the care of hospice. She validated that she was writing a book for terminally ill people about connecting with and expressing their emotions through the process of dying. She cried with joy that her grandfather knew of the writing project, and she was excited about completing it.

Next Marylyn's mom Betty came through to offer her pink roses. Marylyn said those were her mom's favorite flowers. Betty opened up a small tin recipe box (which Marylyn still had) and showed her favorite chocolate brownie recipe. Marylyn was overwhelmed because her mom often made her brownies when she was not feeling well, and she commented that she still had her mom's brownie pan. Betty assured her daughter that they were all with her during her cancer treatments and they would be present to welcome her into spirit when her soul chose to leave the physical body.

Betty communicated that she had passed in and out of consciousness toward the end and she loved the Big Band music they played for her when she was in a coma. She said she often listened to that style of music in her kitchen, which Marylyn confirmed. The pink roses were offered for Marylyn's compassion and comfort to others who would read her healing words.

The next spirit to show up for Marylyn's reading was a gentleman in a Navy uniform with the name Nate. Nate shared a smile and told me to tell Marylyn that nothing in life is by chance. Even the people we meet are significant and come at just the right time. Nate said to remember all the great connections she had made. Marylyn explained that Nate was her commander while she was in the Navy, and he had introduced her to her husband. They often spoke about the importance of being a team in all aspects of life.

Last, but not least, Marylyn's husband Joe presented himself. He talked about her passion for shoes, their morning coffee chats on the patio with matching mugs, playing golf together, and his passion for singing and dancing to the Beach Boys' music. She asked me why he was last to come to the reading. Joe communicated, "Better late than never," and Marylyn giggled on the phone and said Joe had often been late for things.

Joe reminded her of his jar of coins on the dresser and that he had collected wheat pennies. Marylyn confirmed that she had saved his collection of wheat pennies. He encouraged her to enjoy the holidays and to buy new shoes for the New Year's party. Although Marylyn was pleased that her husband came through with his father and she could validate the evidence, she still didn't feel connected to her late husband and hadn't been planning to celebrate the upcoming holiday season. I reminded her that Joe encouraged her to enjoy the holiday and to never miss an opportunity to sing and dance.

Pennies from Heaven

Several weeks later, Marylyn contacted me to let me know her sister insisted Marylyn go shoe shopping and that they spend the holiday together. Halfheartedly, Marylyn found some shoes for New Year's Eve and wore them to her sister's for the holiday. Upon returning to her home the day after New Year's, Marylyn received the ultimate present—a wheat penny found inside her new shoe. As she picked up the penny, she immediately recognized it was from the year 1944, the year Joe was born.

Marylyn slept peacefully with a renewed sense of excitement, knowing that Joe had gifted her with this special penny. When she woke up in the morning, she felt something sticking to her thigh. Another wheat penny was stuck to her leg, letting her know that Joe was with her and loved her. In her mind, she said she heard, "Best wishes for a happy new year from Joe, with pennies from heaven."

Marylyn called for another reading just before her passing. She was very quiet and her sister had to hold the phone up to her ear and help her communicate. I asked her if everything was all right on her side of the phone. I could hear her sniffling, and then she said in all the years she had studied about human consciousness and spirit communication, she never expected to feel so much joy about the afterlife. Marylyn said she loved her life but now she didn't feel worried about crossing over. I just heard her declare over and over, "Dad, I am so blessed. Mom, I am so blessed. Joe I am so blessed." I felt that this was the most loving and enlightening phone call I had experienced in many years.

I communicated that I saw Joe, her parents, and grandparents gathered around her bed and they were already letting her know they were ready to receive her. She whispered into the phone that she saw each one of them, with suitcases, eagerly waiting for her to arrive.

Marylyn's sister Marg had to finish up the phone call. I presented her with comforting messages from her parents, and I let Marg know her parents would take good care of Marylyn on her transition into spirit. Joe asked Marg to bury Marylyn with the penny he sent to her that she found in her shoe. Marg explained that Marylyn had requested that also and hadn't been without the penny since she found it.

We are never alone, and our goodbyes in the physical plane are likened to hellos in the spiritual plane.

GIFTS OF FORGIVENESS

Alex had a very complicated and challenging life. He grew up with an authoritative father who suffered with alcoholism and an unreliable mom who passively looked the other way while his father often beat him. His parents kicked him out of the house before Alex completed high school. He was unable to complete his education because he needed to work to pay for a place to live and food to eat.

With no high school diploma, Alex got a job in construction. His boss was much like his father, abusively authoritative and often hypercritical instead of encouraging with his workers. The boss owned the business and often came to work hung over or drunk. For many years and on many occasions, Alex's paycheck was delayed for weeks at a time. His credit got worse and he lost his car, and his partner at home gave him grief. Money issues caused intense discussions and Alex felt inferior and doubtful about his abilities to provide for his family.

One trying day, Alex learned that his son was gravely ill and needed expensive medications. With a great sense of helplessness and irritation, Alex confronted his boss and demanded he be paid for the four weeks he was owed. A physical altercation occurred and the police were called. Tragically, the police shot and killed Alex as he was beating his boss in his office.

Within a month of Alex's passing, his partner and the mother of his children scheduled a phone consultation to connect with her husband. Before the phone call, I intuitively connected to Sharron's energy and felt a tremendous sense of guilt and hopelessness over her desperate financial situation and abysmal self-esteem.

Sharron began to cry when I told her I felt the presence of someone new to the spirit world with a name that began with "A." I saw him working with a shovel and tools and blueprints, and I felt he passed at a construction site. Essentially, he communicated to me that his death was not an accident. He said he learned to take responsibility for some bad choices and then I saw a police car in my mind. I could not sense the exact manner of his passing, but I felt the tragedy and conflict of a situation related to work.

Alex was still an aggressive spirit and he wanted me to make sure I told Sharron she needed to forgive herself for his passing. As I communicated this to Sharron, I could hear her weep and repeatedly say, "I'm sorry Alex. I'm sorry." She explained that she'd been angry with him for not having the guts to confront his boss about the money they needed for their son and food on the table. Her guilt was overwhelming as she felt her anger caused Alex to have the confrontation with his boss.

To confirm he was aware of her recent problems and concerns, Alex conveyed he knew she was sad for not being able to attend his funeral. He said all four of their children were also heartbroken for not getting to say a proper goodbye. He added that he appreciated the picnic they recently had at their favorite lake in memory of his life. Sharron was greatly relieved that Alex understood why she couldn't attend his service. She explained to me that Alex's parents wouldn't allow her and his own children to go to his funeral because he'd never been properly married.

Alex asked Sharron to forgive his parents because they were annoyed with him for not marrying properly. He said they also felt guilty for not being close to him for most of his life. "Forgiveness will set you free from shame, guilt, and blame," Alex communicated from spirit, and he explained he was working hard to release all remorse; especially involving his parents.

Often, when I do readings, if guilt and resentment exist among family members in conflict, a struggle for the deceased's belongings arises. Typically, guilt tends to embolden family members to want all of the person's belongings, as if to compensate for the loss.

During her reading, Sharron was surprised to learn that Alex had written a will with his attorney and that she needed to get the documentation so she wouldn't lose the house and all his belongings. This pleased and relieved Sharron because she'd recently received a notice from Alex's parents' attorney that she had to leave the house and all his possessions. Alex did ask Sharron to give his parents a few of his items to help compensate for their loss.

Sharron wanted me to ask Alex why they should get *anything* considering they didn't give a damn about him most of his life and had even abused him. Alex's soul had become more aware of its higher self, and he conveyed to her that he wanted to heal from his bad feelings concerning his family and desired for her to heal as well. He explained that each soul is responsible for actions taken and that letting go of the guilt and hatred of his family would help heal her. After all, Alex said, "They can never take our love."

Next, I felt the presence of a warmly nurturing grandmother come from spirit, who was connected to Sharron's mother. She communicated mentally to me that she'd never met Sharron, but she was aware of the challenging relationships she had with her mom and sister—and now Alex's parents. She provided further evidence, confirmed by Sharron, that she had been a dressmaker, had lived in Los Angeles, and had passed from colon cancer in her forties.

Sharron asked why her grandma Beatrice would visit during a reading if she'd never known her. I explained that her grandmother was a part of her soul family, and that many times, relatives who pass when we're children, or even before we're born, choose to be our guardians. As members of our soul family, our loved ones in spirit can best understand our soul agreements and the growth opportunities of our soul.

Grandma Beatrice communicated that because she was from the same soul family, she had challenges similar to Sharron's and she wanted to use this occasion to help her. I felt a stern but reassuring message that Sharron had to stop blaming herself for the shortcomings of her mom and sister and the passing of her husband Alex. Grandma communicated that all souls have the freedom to choose the circumstances and relationships of their life experiences. Sharron had attracted into her life individuals of a like vibration who felt like helpless victims and suffering martyrs.

With great wisdom, Sharron's grandmother reminded her that each person who comes into her life is attracted by her own perceptions and beliefs about who she is. Each person is a teacher, helping her to see herself from a fresh perspective. Grandma reminded Sharron that Alex's family and her mother and sister were all doing the best they could with the self-awareness they had at the moment. Sharron was gifted the wisdom to heal herself by letting go of self-condemnation and empowering herself with the idea that she deserves the very best. Then she would begin to welcome into her life only people who treat her with the same quality of respect.

Initially, Sharron didn't like to be told from her lover and grandmother to let go of the conditioned responses of suffering and self-pity she had about her life. However, several weeks after her reading, she messaged me that she was trying hard to know her innocence and send compassion to those in need. She'd found a hand-carved wooden box with Alex's favorite pocket knife, a photo of him at his work, and a crucifix from his childhood. She mailed these to his parents with a note saying she forgave them and wished them well. Sharron began to heal and grow with a renewed sense of self-respect and confidence. Spirit truly does know what's in the best interest of our soul expansion and growth.

DANNY BOY

Jackson's wife purchased a Skype video reading for her husband, as he had never thought it possible to communicate with the dead. I explained the procedure to Jackson, and he replied I would have to prove spirit communication to him because he was highly suspicious. As I explain to all my clients, I am not here to prove my abilities or the existence of the spirit world. Through the experience of the reading, sitters can come to their own conclusion. That said, I was thinking, oh geez—another challenging skeptic. I hoped to provide verifiable evidence and insightful messages to inspire Jackson's mind.

Directly, an older gentleman wearing a jumpsuit and holding wrenches appeared in my mind's eye. He was in a garage, with Elvis Presley music on the radio, and he was working on engines. He telepathically communicated that he'd never met Jackson, he was a grandfather on his dad's side, and he had died of a heart condition. This seemed pretty amazing to Jackson. He confirmed that his paternal grandfather had passed when his dad was young from a sudden heart attack and that he'd assembled engines in a factory. Also, Jackson remembers his dad telling him that he and his father had shared their love of listening to Elvis Presley.

Jackson's grandpa then presented his father, who was with him in spirit. Attentively, Jackson listened for evidence. Jackson's father shared that he'd left suddenly in an accident and hadn't been able to say goodbye to his family. I felt his chest was compressed and a sadness for leaving so quickly. Jackson asked me to provide his dad's name. I didn't get his name and told Jackson I could only provide the information that was sent to me. His dad showed me a small airplane and said he loved to fly. This brought Jackson to tears because his father had gotten his small-plane pilot's license and he loved to go on short trips with rented planes. Then, I saw a wooden cabin on a lake, with a dock and a small fishing boat. Again, tears filled Jackson's eyes, as every summer his family vacationed at such a place and his dad and Jackson enjoyed fishing together.

His father communicated he was pleased that Jackson had taken care of his mother and that someone had just moved. Jackson explained that last week he had moved his mom into an assisted living community so she could remain active and have others close by to look in on her. Jackson's father communicated with laughter how "fun" it was to get mom to downsize all her ceramic figures and formal plates. Jackson confirmed that this was the most challenging variable in getting his mom to move.

Jackson was encountering people connected to restoring old planes, as his dad had enjoyed, he said, and he would have such conversations in the most random places. I asked him how these conversations made him feel, and he smiled and said he knew that somehow they were associated with his dad. Also, Jackson shared that Elvis music would be playing in random stores and shops or on his radio on a regular basis. He asked if this was just because he missed his dad, and I said it felt as though his dad wanted his attention.

A short older lady came through with a sun hat on, carrying a spade, and she showed me tulips and roses. I felt she was a grandma energy and she was good at canning what she grew in her backyard garden. I saw a "G" on her apron. Jackson smiled as he realized this was his maternal grandma Gladys. I got the strong scent of lilacs, and Jackson remembered that her backyard was full of lilac bushes and that his grandma loved her tulip garden. Gladys conveyed that she was proud of Jackson for being so kind to his mother and for being a good husband. I saw a biplane and a tall slender man standing next to Grandma in my mind. Jackson explained that his grandpa had flown a biplane in the war, and he was the one who encouraged Jackson's dad to fly.

With a stunned expression, Jackson said he couldn't believe how he felt the presence of his family in spirit during the reading. He explained he'd been a total skeptic before the reading, but now he knew that his loved ones were with him.

He asked if his father approved of his career. At first, I heard the occupations architect and designer, and in my mind, I saw blueprints with rulers and other measuring devices on a drafting table. Jackson's expression on the monitor was priceless. His current job was designing boats, but he was attending classes to learn more about architecture. This was the validation he was hoping would come from the reading. The images of blueprints and small wooden houses in the woods were presented by Jackson's dad clairvoyantly. I heard that Jackson blended his analytical design mind with his artistic skill designing homes in nature. "Oh, my gosh!" I remember Jackson yelling. He and his wife were starting a business of designing small vacation homes in the wilderness. He explained that they'd just completed their first design, and he wanted to leave his job to do this full time. Then I heard Jackson's father say he loved the new floors. With a big grin, Jackson affirmed his father's message, saying he and his wife had just finished the wooden floors in their new cabin.

The reading was helpful for Jackson in giving him confidence to pursue his passion of designing small wilderness homes. His father closed the reading by explaining to his son that the choice was his, and his choices would determine the quality of his life experiences.

As Jackson was processing his messages, I reminded him that success in life comes from manifesting from passion. The more Jackson enjoyed what he did, the greater would be his quality of life. Passion attracts people, situations, and experiences that will improve every aspect of the quality of life, as spirit often communicates.

Now I felt Jackson was waiting to hear from someone else, and he looked a bit worried that this spirit wouldn't visit for the reading. A younger male spirit appeared in my mind, and he was holding a tennis racket and balls. I heard him say, "Tell dad, game is on." Now

Jackson wept for a short time before I could share more. His wife appeared behind him on the monitor and hugged him and told him it would be all right.

Telepathically, I heard the song "Old Danny Boy," and Jackson confirmed his son was named Danny and he often called him Danny Boy. Danny was persistent in showing me the tennis racquet and balls. He seemed to be encouraging his dad to play tennis. It was hard for Jackson to communicate because his passion was tennis and he'd played almost every Saturday with Danny. He said he'd been unable to even watch tennis since Danny's passing. Cunningly, though, Danny communicated that his dad would feel his presence more if they shared the sport they were most passionate about. "Please promise you will play again," Danny asked me to share with his dad.

Jackson explained he had so much anger that his son had been taken away from him, that even two years after his passing, he felt lost, hopeless, and sad. Danny showed me that he'd been in a car accident but he hadn't been driving the car. He told his dad to forgive the driver, that he hadn't been in pain, and he was now able to help lots of young people in the spirit world. Jackson was still shaken up and told me his son had been killed by another student, who'd been driving under the influence of alcohol and drugs.

I felt Thanksgiving was extra special to Danny, and his father mentioned it was around the time of his birthday. I saw photos of Danny winning awards for tennis and running. Jackson proudly shared that his son had gone to All State for tennis and had won a college scholarship for tennis. He'd also been on the cross-country team and won many awards in high school. One last time, Danny reminded his father to play tennis so he would feel more connected to him and he would be playing the sport they both loved so passionately.

Several months later, I received an email from Jackson, and he wanted to thank his son, dad, and grandmother for sharing such life-changing messages. He told me he'd reluctantly joined a tennis league but now was enjoying it very much. He wrote that he felt the presence of his son and that he and his wife had purchased tickets to the US Open for the fall, which is a trip they'd made several times with Danny.

Our loved ones are incredibly supportive in helping us understand the healing that's necessary for us to find more satisfaction and joy in our lives. Jackson rediscovered his passion on the tennis court and his purpose in building cabins. He said he still felt sadness each day, but he knew he would feel his dad each time he was constructing a home and his son every time he aced his tennis serve. Love is the question, the answer, and the truth.

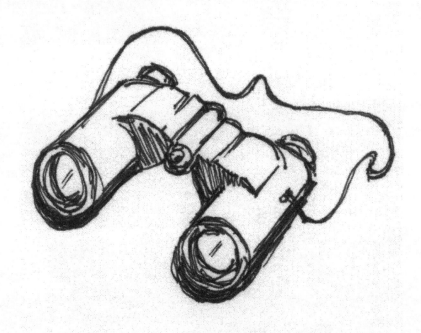

ROSES FROM SYLVIA

Her memories began to fall away from her mind in her eighty-fifth year, like the aged rose petals in her garden. Though the tranquil remembrance of her elegant garden of bright roses with its sweet smells and dancing butterflies couldn't be erased, she could no longer recall her own name.

Sylvia created a garden to overcome her sorrows from the passing of her son Billy, who'd been killed defending his nation during the Korean War, and the loss of her beloved husband Stan, whose heart had stopped just before their forty-fourth wedding anniversary.

The five decades of dedication to her comforting friends, her roses, was a testament to her devotion to the men she loved in spirit. Vibrant but soft orange roses were in devotion to her son with his enthusiastic personality and red hair. Deep red roses symbolized the profound love she shared with her beloved Stan. After all, Stan was a lifetime Red Socks fan and red was his favorite color to wear.

Margaret, Sylvia's mom, had been a master gardener and influenced Sylvia's passion for gardening. Sylvia often thought of her mom with her cream and ivory roses and had often teased her about adding more colorful blossoms. But her mom believed that her hues of white were heavenly and pure.

When the frosty chill of winter filled the air and her pruned rose bushes were prepared for their winter slumber, Sylvia took her final breath and crossed into spirit. In the following spring, Sylvia's daughters came for a reading.

Initially, Grandma Margaret, Sylvia's mom, visited during the reading. Grandma presented her love of roses and the matching Easter dresses she had sewn for the sisters when they were in grade school. The sisters commented how they'd just found Easter photographs at Grandma Margaret's house and they all had matching yellow floral dresses, with matching purses and white gloves.

Grandma wanted to assure the sisters that their mom was with her in the spirit world. Sylvia communicated to the daughters that her name began with an "S" and that she had had dementia for several years before passing. She thanked her daughters for the care they had provided and the joy of being able to spend her final days at her home, near her garden.

Sylvia wanted her daughters to know she was with their father and brother in the spirit world, and they all often visited one another. She communicated that the three of them in spirit were each watching out for their four children. Sylvia completed her communication with the idea that her sign of love, support, and encouragement would always be a rose. The scent of rose or the visual presentation of a rose was Mom's way to say, "I love you and I am always with you." Sylvia said she would make sure her girls received roses on special occasions by intuitively inspiring their family members to purchase them.

A young male spirit presented himself and he impressed in my mind the visual of a baseball field and a red baseball hat. I saw him pitching, and his sisters commented that their brother Billy had mostly played pitcher and shortstop. He also showed me himself wearing a green uniform. He was holding a gun and was in a tent. I felt as though he'd been killed in the war because he showed me the American flag at half mast, and I saw rows and rows of white granite graves. The sisters confirmed that Billy had been killed in the Korean War.

They asked their brother if he had any messages for them and if he had met Mom and Dad in spirit. Billy acknowledged that two of the sisters each had a son and he was their guardian. He communicated that both boys were outstanding athletes and he was proud of them. He conveyed his support for his youngest sister, who had recently been divorced and asked her to let her other sisters help her choose a kinder husband in the future.

Billy then brought through their father Stan from spirit. He telepathically shared his love of birding and showed me binoculars. The sisters all smiled as they each had a pair of his binocular as reminders of him. The symbolic message in regards to the binoculars, Stan shared, was to always see the difficulties of day-to-day life from afar to give a more realistic perspective on things. He also wisely communicated that life is all about one's own viewpoint.

I could smell pipe tobacco and saw in my mind a small man with black-rimmed glasses sitting in an easy chair doing crossword puzzles. Also, I saw a bag of potato chips. Again, the girls all laughed and confirmed their dad's passion for relaxing in his chair, working on the daily crossword puzzle, and smoking his pipe. Their father's favorite snack was chips, and they even left bags at his grave every now and then.

Sylvia shared her happiness that she was reconnected with the two men she loved the most and how much easier life was in spirit. Symbolically, she presented each daughter with a red and an orange rose, which confirmed the two main types of roses she had in her garden. She also acknowledged to her daughters that she often sat on a bench in her garden and read poetry to the two men she had missed the most.

The sisters explained that their mom would often sit on a bench and read poetry and romance novels. Their mom also encouraged her daughters to sell her home and not feel guilty or bad about their decision. The girls were glad their mom brought up the topic of selling her home. They had debated a lot about what to do with it, and the girls wished they could keep the rose garden for its sentimental value and beauty. Sylvia told her daughters to each take some of her rose bushes to plant in their own gardens and then they'd feel most connected to her.

Several years later, one of the sisters returned for a reading. She was so happy the signs and symbols her loved ones shared in the reading she'd had with her two sisters were so prevalent and arrived just at the right moment. The one sign that most impressed the sisters was how mom's bushes all seemed to bloom at the same time, even though all three sisters lived miles apart. Sylvia was communicating through her passionate roses that she truly was with each daughter.

THE INFORMATION BOOTH

The airport loudspeaker suddenly blasted, "Aaron Jacobs, Aaron Jacobs, please come to the information booth to receive an important message." With disbelief and a sense of excitement, Carl and Renee immediately scrambled to the information booth because this was their deceased son's name . . . but how could it be? To their surprise, they met a young lady carrying a guitar case with short blonde hair and a bright smile. Carl and Renee introduced themselves to Erin, and they couldn't believe how much she looked like their son—especially her steel-blue eyes. Even her mannerisms were quite similar with her laid-back demeanor and humble stance.

Erin explained she was traveling from her home in Montana to perform some of her new music in Nashville. Renee began to cry, and Carl explained the unique coincidence of their son Aaron. To make matters even more remarkable, Erin had the same kind of leather bracelet as their son Aaron, and she also composed blues-style music with her guitar, just as Aaron had done.

Renee's son had encouraged her to go on this trip during her reading with me just months earlier. After their trip, I received a phone call from Renee, and she explained the miraculous sign she'd received from Aaron from the spirit world at the Montana airport.

Three months before Renee's trip to Montana, she'd hired me for a mediumship reading because of the heavy grief and deep sadness she felt due to two recent deaths in her immediate family. As I convened with Renee, I saw in my mind the presence of a father with a fishing pole and net, wearing hip boots and a unique fishing hat, which I described as like the one Indian Jones wore in the movies. Nodding with a tear-streaked face, Renee acknowledged that this must be her father Eddie. Her father mentally showed me a pocket knife and white handkerchiefs with a "W" on them. With astonishment, Renee pulled out the pocket knife, which she carried with her. She explained that her father always had his white hankies with a "W" on them for his last name, Williams.

Renee clarified that her father often went on fishing trips wearing the clothing I described, and he'd left her his favorite fishing knife. Just as a pocket knife is a resourceful tool, Eddie reminded his daughter that she was the most ingenious and practical human being he knew.

It was important for Renee to hear the message that her father was pleased with how she took care of his estate, and that it was rational for her to sell his home. Renee was relieved to hear that her father approved of this sale, because she felt guilt-ridden for letting it go.

Eddie said he had a "son" with him in spirit who had passed because of an unexpected accident. I asked Renee if she had a brother or a son in spirit. Renee froze with shock and said that her dad was bringing through her son. The younger male presented himself with bandages around his head and showed me the month of January on a calendar. Surprised and calmer, Renee confirmed that her son had passed just a few months earlier, in January, and had died from a head injury from falling off a balcony.

This young spirit showed me turntables and old record albums. I heard him say "twenty-six," and he asked me to tell his mom he's "chill." Laughing, Renee affirmed by eagerly nodding her head. She explained that her son owned his own DJ business; he spun his 45s on the old turntables, and played music at events. He was twenty-six when he passed. She kept grinning from his comment about being "chill," as he'd often told her that.

I could hear a name with an "Ar" sound, and Renee explained

that her son's name was Aaron, and he composed music with his guitar, which he never left home without.

Using my clairaudience, I could hear Aaron say that November was an important month and that he wanted her to go on the fishing trip with Dad. Renee explained that Carl was actually a stepdad to Aaron, but the most meaningful father figure to him, and they often had an annual salmon fishing trip together. Carl and Aaron had airline tickets and a cabin reserved for a fishing trip to Montana that November to celebrate both of their birthdays.

I could also hear Aaron sing a blues-like style of music with his guitar, and Renee confirmed that he wrote blues music and played in a blues band. He communicated that his mom would find a great sense of peace by going on the fishing trip, and that she would know he was there with her. She kept saying she was in too much pain and didn't feel she could travel until her grief lessened. I could feel Aaron's perseverance and he asked me to please tell his mom to go and she would heal and be inspired by the events of the trip. As I shared this message with Renee, she continued to weep and shake her head no.

As a medium, I'm just the messenger for communications from loved ones, and at times I feel frustrated with my inability to convey the significance of certain messages. Just as when sharing messages from people in the physical plane, recipients can hear but they don't always listen.

Renee asked me to explain how she would know her son was still with her. I shared the wisdom gifted to me in readings that spirits creatively use numerous but ordinary methods to reassure their loved ones they are present. One of the most common methods to present messages is through dreams, because we're most open to receive in the astral plane of sleep. I often refer to visitations from the spirit world when someone is dreaming, and many times, spirits can essentially hug, kiss, or touch you in a dream.

I explained to Renee that spirits are very artistic and persistent in using nature to communicate to loved ones. Butterflies, dragonflies, ladybugs, or specific birds can fly into your path at just the divine right moment. Spirits might bring to your awareness heart-shaped stones, feathers, pennies, or certain flowers. They're also ingenious at presenting scents, such as a favorite flower, perfume or cologne, or odors associated with a food they liked, a hobby, or their work.

Aaron let me know he was skilled with electronics, and he gets his mom's attention by switching the radio station, flickering the lights, or calling his cell phone. Renee confirmed that many times his cell phone rings with an unknown caller and she feels it's her son calling just when she's feeling sad. This type of messaging is also common with many other spirits, I've discovered.

In my mind, I saw guitar picks, sheet music, old 45s, and dragonflies. Aaron was sharing with his mom specific signs that she could associate with him. Of course, any blues style of music would be an attention-getter, but because my knowledge of this style of music is limited, I couldn't offer a particular artist. Renee commented that she was still finding Aaron's guitar picks in strange places, and she had a feeling her son was saying hello in his intimate way.

Renee then remarked that on her last camping trip with Aaron, they had come across a pond in a huge mountain meadow with hundreds of dancing dragonflies. As she thought more about it, she realized that dragonflies often appeared on her porch when she was reading. I informed Renee that the dragonfly is a water symbol for transformation of the higher mind. It makes sense that Aaron would choose the dragonfly as a sign because he loved being around the water, plus he'd been studying about human consciousness for years.

You can imagine how stunned and euphoric Renee was the morning she received the astonishing message from her son Aaron at the Montana airport through Erin. Look what she would have missed had she not finally "listened" and gone on the trip. Not only did Renee meet a new musical friend, but she knew the consciousness of her son lived on. I told her that her story was extraordinary and noted how creative her son was to use an "information" booth in an airport to share the most valuable news: Life is continuous and love is forever. Nothing is a coincidence; everything is perfectly orchestrated with the assistance of our loved ones in spirit.

GRACE AND HOPE

Gail learned about my abilities and services when she represented the seller for the home I purchased. Shortly after the real estate transaction, Jean, her partner of over forty years, passed away from lung disease. As I'd never met the seller or the seller's agent, I didn't know who Gail was when she showed up for her reading.

As I meditated and started connecting with Gail's loved ones, I felt the presence of a mother vibration who had had cancer in her digestive system and I felt that Gail had cared for her. I could hear an "R" sound, and saw a short, stout lady, smoking cigarettes, eating donuts, and wearing a mumu. In my mind, I could hear a very raspy voice with lots of foul language but great humor. Gail verified that her mother Loraine, whom they called Rae, had passed several years ago from lung cancer and Gail had been her primary caregiver.

Another older female spirit presented herself, and she telepathically communicated that she had had memory issues before her passing and she was thankful she was cared for by her family. She said to thank Gail for helping her out. She showed me old TV shows in black and white, such as *I Love Lucy*, *The Munsters*, *I Dream of Jeannie*, and *Bewitched*. Gail smiled, saying these were her mother-in-law Alice's favorite shows. She asked how I could know these shows so specifically. I explained that her loved one Alice could impress upon me the shows we knew in common so I could provide specific evidence.

Alice communicated that she had loved her ice cream sundaes

and she was at peace now that she had her mind back. Every Saturday night, Gail confirmed with tears, she'd made Alice's recipe for peanut butter and chocolate hot fudge sundae sauce, and they watched old TV shows.

Because of her constant kindness, Alice wanted to surprise Gail and bring through her soul mate and wife, Jean. Gail began to weep, and I immediately felt this was the main reason she'd come to get a reading. Before parting, Alice reminded Gail they were with her every day and watched over her.

As I began to blend with Jean, I felt great loving kindness toward Gail, and she impressed in my mind that she was very bright and loved to read. I could see a chalkboard, an apple, and literature books in my mind's eye, and Gail smiled with tears, saying that Jean had been a college literature professor. With more detail, Jean showed me the names Ernest Hemmingway and Mark Twain, and Gail explained that these were her favorite authors to share and teach in her classes.

At times I'm shown objects or specific items and I don't completely understand what spirit is trying to communicate, but I do the best I can at sharing the impressions. Jean showed me a green glass box, which I mentally opened and saw three pennies inside. I was also shown a turtle and Hawaii on a map. I felt these items offered many layers of meaning and asked Gail to help me understand. Gail explained they had taken annual trips to Maui and that Jean loved turtles, but she didn't understand the message. I asked her to take it with her and it would make more sense in time.

Jean showed me herself and her mom Alice sitting on the screened-in porch of what looked like a log cabin, and they were watching the sunset over a lake. They were playing Scrabble and chess. From her facial expressions and body language, I knew this hit home with Gail. She explained that this sounded like Alice's lake house, which the girls often visited, and that Scrabble was Jean's favorite game. Gail said she has Jean's Scrabble board and often feels her presence connected to it.

Jean asked Gail to give her dogs a hug. I saw large black dogs and Gail confirmed they have two black labs and she can tell they're depressed now that Jean is gone. Jean communicated that the dogs, Hope and Grace, still sit between the matching recliners in the den. Jean conveyed that she loved that Gail wore her orange shirt. Again, Gail was in tears and said that Jean loved Syracuse University, and she often wore her orange jersey.

I felt the presence of a younger male come through, and I heard the name Eddie. Jean told me mentally to let Eddie's family know he's with her. Eddie telepathically told me to please tell his family he's safe now. Gail seemed confused because the only Eddie she knew was her cousin's son. She asked if maybe it was Edward, her grandfather. I asked her if they called him Eddie and if he'd passed in his twenties. She replied that her grandfather was very old when he died, and she didn't remember anyone calling him Eddie.

Gail decided to schedule another in-person session two months later. She was eager to share insights from her first readings, and she showed me two full pages of questions she had for more information. But first, Gail asked me to connect to whatever spirit would like to come through.

Instantly, I felt her partner Jean, and Jean communicated that their dogs were helping Gail find the clues she was leaving around the house. Gail reminded me of the labs Grace and Hope, and I thought how appropriate the names were for these canine messengers.

Tears trickled down Gail's face, and she smiled saying, "I knew it; I knew our babies were connected to Jean." With such assurance, Jean shared that the dogs had led her to the green glass turtle box one night when she was crying hysterically, really missing Jean. The box was on Jean's bookshelf in her office and had been a gift from their good friends for Jean because she couldn't travel to Maui on the annual trip because of her illness. When Gail opened the box, she was astonished to find three pennies inside, as I'd seen in my mind in her last reading. It makes my heart smile when a sitter appreciates and fully embraces the loving messages from spirit.

The literal aspect of the message was discovered, but now I asked Gail to work with me on determining the symbolic meaning of the turtle box and the pennies. Jean helped by impressing in my mind that turtles represent the concept that you take your home with you wherever you go. Jean was communicating that home is wherever you are, and she would always be with Gail, so in essence, she was home.

In my mind, I could hear Frank Sinatra singing "Three Coins in the Fountain" and shared this with Gail. She dropped her papers on the floor and gasped, saying that the movie *Three Coins in the Fountain* was one of their all-time favorite movies, and they had watched it every year. She also said that Frank Sinatra was one of Jean's favorite musicians, and she had bought many of his albums.

The profound meaning of the turtle box and the three pennies as a sign from Jean was tremendously healing to Gail. This illustrated that when the medium, sitter, and spirit work together, the significance of spirit communications can be comprehended and bring great joy.

Before Gail departed, after receiving other messages from loved ones, she reminded me that in her last reading a young male, Eddie, had come through with Jean and said he was all right. After her first reading, Gail learned that her cousin's son had taken his life the day before her first reading, and she had not yet been aware of it. We both were in awe that Eddie could be heard from spirit so soon after passing, but he was determined to let his family know he had crossed and was safe.

Gail asked if Eddie had any other messages that would help her cousin Betty heal from the loss of her son. Eddie showed me crows, and I could hear cawing in my head. Gail said she had a recent phone call with Betty, who said that every morning crows showed up on the front porch and she felt it was a sign from her son.

Eddie impressed in my mind model racecars and a checkered flag. Once again, Gail confirmed these messages with tears and explained that Eddie had loved to work on racecars. In his bedroom were old model race cars from his younger years and a flag he received from working with a racecar team. I explained that the checkered flag held the symbolic meaning that Eddie had made it to the finish line.

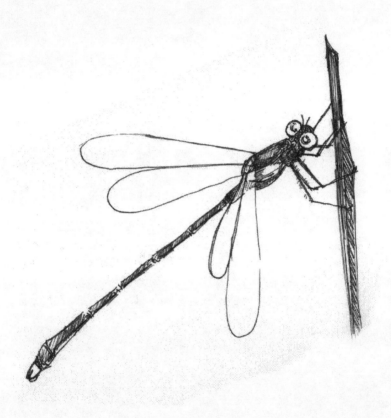

YOU CAN'T KILL YOURSELF

Your true SELF is your divine and sacred spirit. It temporarily borrows your body when your spirit incarnates into the physical plane. The physical body also holds the ego-mind and can be thought of as a "costume" specially selected by your spirit to complement the karma your spirit hopes to comprehend and heal.

The spirit survives the death of the physical body and gathers and stores your experiences, truths, and karma. Your consciousness and awareness of yourself is part of your spirit as well. Death is determined by when the physical body can no longer maintain biological functions and the spirit leaves the body. Even if medical apparatus still regulates the body's functions, the spirit can be gone—or stuck, waiting nearby for the body to "give up the ghost."

One of the most incomprehensible experiences is when a loved one takes his or her own life. Many doors lead from the physical world to the spiritual, but the most complicated and deeply emotional death is suicide.

Eckhart Tolle points out a basic truth with the statement from his book *Stillness Speaks:* "Wherever you go, there you are." When individuals end their physical life, they carry their consciousness with them into the world of spirit. Despite their wishes, there's no escape from the depression, anxiety, hopelessness, and helplessness they may feel, even after leaving the physical plane. The karma they created by taking their life can be distressingly intense as well, for their spirit will have to feel all the pain and suffering they caused all those who loved them.

A CASE OF SUICIDE

Maureen had suffered with many losses throughout her lifetime and wanted a reading to try to understand why her soul chose such a difficult path. I could sense the tremendous guilt, grief, and pain she harbored and asked spirits to come forth to help her heal.

Initially, I felt the presence of a man in his early forties and heard the name Bob. He expressed his fear of loving others, showed me liquor and pill bottles, and was sitting on a picnic table on a back porch. He communicated that he had taken his own life in the garage with a gun when Maureen was in grade school. Maureen was paralyzed and shocked that her father was visiting her. She validated the information, remembering that her dad always sat on the back porch and had substance abuse issues.

Bob then brought forth a younger but taller male in coveralls, holding a wrench, toolbox, and buckets. He was smoking a cigarette, and I could hear Pink Floyd and The Cars playing. Immediately Maureen identified him as her husband Rick. She cried with relief knowing that Rick had come to visit with her. She confirmed the music he played while he worked as a plumber. She also said that often she could still smell his cigarette smoke when she was missing him. He showed me a dragonfly, and Maureen lifted her sleeve to show the dragonfly tattoo she'd gotten in his memory.

Rick communicated that he was sorry he'd taken his life, but he'd felt hopeless and depressed for not being able to provide for his family. He was pleased Maureen had moved away from the house where he took his life. He conveyed through clairaudience that the dragonfly was a significant and appropriate symbol because it represented a change in consciousness. Rick shared that he and Maureen were working on shifting their awareness away from pain and suffering.

Maureen asked how he was doing and if he had found peace

of mind yet. Rick acknowledged that he'd been gone for only a few years, and he was still working on overcoming his lower thoughts of depression. He then communicated something very important for me to convey to her and an idea new to my consciousness. Recognizing the grief and guilt Maureen was experiencing, Rick said the more happiness Maureen could generate for herself, the more efficiently *he* could heal. Likewise, as he learned to be more at peace, he said he could help her to overcome her sadness. In other words, two connected souls in different planes of existence can deeply influence each other's healing and spiritual growth. True synergy.

In terms of connection, I realized how important it is for sitters to perceive the circumstances of a loved one's passing and heal themselves. The more Maureen could overcome her emotions of fear, separation, sadness, and hopelessness and heal thoughts of guilt and shame, the more easily she could feel Rick's presence. Spirits exist in a higher vibration than those on the earth plane, even when they're recovering from suicide. Sorrow, grief, and depression further lower awareness and vibration, while love, peace, and joy enhance the ability to connect with the higher awareness of the spirit plane. Healing and a rise in vibration on either side will enhance connection.

Maureen asked if another male in spirit wished to communicate. In my mind, I saw a black journal with charcoal drawings, a stuffed monkey, posters of music bands from the 70s, and a blue backpack filled with books of poetry. The room was dark and I sensed Maureen sitting on the bed, often crying. She explained that this was her son's room and everything was correct, except it was a stuffed dog on the bed, not a monkey. I could distinctly hear the name Junior as he felt more comfortable communicating with me.

I saw a tall, lean teenager with long hair, and he was wearing a gray hoodie. He communicated that he appreciated I was helping his mom and wanted to speak to her about his passing. Junior said he was sorry he took his own life and realized how selfish he'd been to his mom and sisters for leaving without a word. He explained he'd lost his job and failed his college classes, and his girlfriend had left him. He asked Momo (what he called his mom, Maureen) to forgive him for not appreciating how much she and his sisters loved him.

Maureen wept with me as we both felt the incredible healing moment that miraculously just happened. She said, "Please help me release the most troubling question of why. *Why?*" Junior said he made the mistake of constantly comparing himself academically and athletically to his friends and his sisters, but he was learning how to love and appreciate himself in spirit. He communicated that his awareness in the spirit world was much different because judgment, self-punishment, and shame disappear. He wanted to assure Momo that he was surrounded by affectionately kind beings who love him.

I saw a large flock of crows and heard them in my mind cawing. Junior also showed me a beautiful flowering magnolia tree with a small bench beneath it. Maureen smiled through her cleansing tears, as she explained that she had buried both her husband's and son's ashes under the magnolia tree and she often sat on the bench beneath the tree to communicate with them. The crows were an important sign to her also, as she often saw two crows, Rick and Rick Jr., fly in her path.

In my gut I felt cautious, as Rick Jr. expressed his concern for his younger sister, and Maureen confirmed she was struggling with the passing of her dad and brother. Debbie was in high school and had trouble getting close to people. She happened to be sitting in the room with her mom, and Junior asked her to please know that love is safe and that their father and he would help her to heal her heart. I could hear her cry over the phone and her brother said he was aware that she kept a pair of her dad's and his socks in her nightstand, and she had a wooden box under her bed where she kept ribbons and memorable photographs of them. Debbie validated her brother's message, and he reassured her that love was not only harmless, but love was her purpose for being. Junior told her she was a natural healer and he supported her desire to be a psychotherapist.

Maureen then told me she'd been to another medium who had said that her father, husband, and son were stuck in purgatory for taking their own lives. She was most concerned that her loved ones were being punished and their spirits were being held back. I explained that spirits aren't judged by the standards of the world, and that souls learn to forgive themselves and heal. The only time a soul gets held back is when it's within the physical body with the ego-mind. I reminded both Maureen and Debbie that their thoughts and feelings could be either supportive or limiting with regard to the progression of their loved ones' souls.

Rick and Rick Jr. wanted Maureen and her daughters to know they loved them more than ever and felt the love their family sent to them. They asked them to be open to the affectionate thoughts they sent and avowed they would help each other to release their sadness and celebrate their spirits.

Almost one year later, Maureen and her two daughters traveled to see me for an in-person reading. Like old acquaintances, I felt both Ricks come through during the reading and they felt lighter and brighter, as did the ladies. All three ladies had implemented Junior's advice and they celebrated the lives they shared with their father/ husband and brother/son. Junior commended them for starting a suicide survivors' empowerment group and communicated how pleased he was they had helped so many people surrender their guilt and grief and open their hearts to love.

Both Ricks shared that they were able to heal and expand their consciousness with the tremendous help of these ladies. They were connecting with spirits who had taken their lives and were family members of the suicide survivors' empowerment group the ladies had started. How simply amazing it is that this family, living in two separate planes, is still united and all helping members of the same soul family. As our loved ones in spirit guide us, we can also be guides to their enlightenment. Life and the afterlife interact in an eternal collaboration of loving kindness.

WHEN IS THE RIGHT TIME TO GO?

Donald was a very nervous and angry husband, brother, and father. His own insecurities pushed his ego to try to control all aspects of his family life. In the work environment, he was unable to make choices because of the authoritative nature of the factory leadership. The only way he could get attention at the large manufacturing company was through increasing outputs, decreasing expenses, or selling more products.

When Donald anxiously returned home from work each evening, he took out his self-doubt and frustration in feeling insecure on his wife Laura and stepdaughter Anna. No matter how Laura and Anna tried to appease Donald, he was bossy and critical of them. He didn't like the clothes they wore and how the table was set, the beef wasn't tender enough, and on and on. Donald always dished out plenty of hostility.

Sally, Donald's sister, phoned him one evening to share the sad news that their mother had suffered a severe heart attack and would most likely not survive the night. True to his mean-spirited character, he chewed his sister out on the phone for not calling him sooner and insisted she give him all the power to make decisions. Unable to get to the hospital before his mother passed, he aggressively yelled at the hospital staff and his sister for not keeping her alive long enough for him to get there. His sister reminded him that their mother had a Do Not Resuscitate order, as did he, although he just criticized her for not caring for Mom better and tried to guilt her into feeling even worse.

Even though Sally was to organize their mom's services per their mother's request, Donald insisted he would make all the arrangements. Sally provided the written instructions from Mom, including a request for cremation and a celebration of life service. Donald disagreed and allowed his ego-mind to control the situation, arranging for a formal funeral service and burial in the plot next to their father.

Several years later, Sally scheduled a phone reading because her brother Donald had had a major stroke, had been resuscitated twice against his request, and was on life support. Sally's mother came through strongly during her reading and confirmed her identity by sharing that she'd had a heart attack, had been on life support, and had been given a formal funeral, of which she hadn't approved. Sally was relieved to know her mom, in spirit, was familiar with her lack of choices given her brother's insistence.

Interestingly, Sally's mom said her brother Donald had one foot in the door of the spirit world and had visited her in spirit. She communicated that Donald had had a debilitating stroke, which Sally confirmed to me. Sally didn't understand why her brother hadn't passed, even though his heart had stopped two times that week. Sally's mom shared inspiring wisdom about Donald's soul agreement. Like his entire soul family, Donald had come into this lifetime with the soul agreement to let go of low self-esteem and the sense of being powerless, and align more with confidence, empowerment, and greater self-worth.

Laura and Anna couldn't decide to remove life support because during most of their experience with Donald, they hadn't been allowed to make choices unless he approved. Sally's mom said the karma Donald created from always being in charge and taking choice away from his wife and stepdaughter was being healed by his soul being powerless in this challenging situation. The ladies' soul lesson, a final gift from Donald, was a rare but welcomed option: to exercise their free will to make a choice. The powerless wife and stepdaughter, who had devoted their lives to encouraging and supporting Donald's mean-spirited influence in their lives, now had all the power to decide when it was time for Donald to go.

Several months later, Sally brought her sister-in-law Laura to have a reading together. The first spirit to communicate was Sally's father Randy. Randy thanked Sally and Laura for taking care of him at the end of his life, and he especially enjoyed the foot rubs and classical music they played for him. I could feel heaviness in the lungs and challenges breathing, and Sally acknowledged that her father had passed from emphysema and that she and Laura had taken turns watching him, with the care of hospice the last few months of his life.

Clairvoyantly, I could see a telescope and then notebooks filled with complex mathematical formulas. I saw many journals on Randy's desk and a calculator. Laura spoke this time and said that her father-in-law had been an aerospace engineer and he was published in numerous scientific journals. I also saw a leather bomber jacket and asked Sally if this meant something to her. She cried and explained that this was the only item she had from her father.

Randy wanted to apologize for not being involved in Sally's life and for distancing himself from the family. He realized, after reflecting on his life, that his devotion to his work had prevented him from spending time with his family. Although he'd been a highly successful aerospace engineer, he had not been a supportive dad.

Sally's father then wanted to bring through another male spirit, and I could hear the name Dan or Don. Both ladies' eyes filled with tears and acknowledged that Donald was Sally's brother and Laura's husband. I got the strong feeling that Donald regretted having been bossy and mean-spirited to both of these ladies. He impressed in my mind to please tell them both he was sorry and that he was learning to forgive his dad as he spent time with him in the spirit world.

Donald showed me a factory environment with many machines. I saw him sitting at a desk and looking over reports and files, and I was shown he was a supervisor. Both of the ladies nodded to show me they understood the messages.

Laura asked if he was okay. Donald replied that he was working on controlling his thoughts and emotions, and he wanted Laura to know she did the right thing to sign the papers to let him go. He kept apologizing for his demeaning behavior and wanted Laura to know he loved her and was happy she'd gotten a job related to money or finances. As if a dam had been opened, Laura's eyes flooded with tears of relief. She'd harbored immense guilt about whether she should have signed the papers to take him off life support. She also explained to me that after twenty years, she had returned to being a bank teller.

Donald communicated to Sally that he was proud of all she'd done to support his family and their parents. He admitted he was always intimidated by her sense of power and ability to be decisive throughout her life. He also confessed he was still learning how to heal his insecurities relating to her confidence and self-reliance. Donald asked me to convey to Sally that their mom was helping him to be more gracious and thoughtful.

Laura asked if Donald had any messages for Anna, his stepdaughter. In my heart, I could feel Donald had great thoughtfulness for Anna. He communicated that he sends Anna hearts in all forms, including clouds, puddles, and rocks. He said he was pleased Anna had gotten a divorce and hoped she would find someone less like him. In my mind, I saw textbooks and the scales of justice, and I sensed Anna must be in school associated with the legal profession. Laura was pleased to know that Donald supported Anna's decisions to divorce her abusive husband and start college to become a paralegal.

Donald perceptively let Sally and Laura know that timing is divine and sacred in each moment and decision of their lives. He asked them to be mindful and aware of each choice of thought, word, deed, or action because each had equivalent consequences. He added that as he grew to understand more, he would impress ideas into their minds.

Last, he shared the realization that control of our thoughts and feelings is the only real power our souls have, but it's the only power we need to know our true self. Both ladies replied how happy they were about the progression of Donald's soul, and that they would take his messages to heart.

THE SHIFT

Perception is a choice. How you choose to perceive will determine the quality of your life experience, whether your spirit is within the physical body or a "free" spirit. *A Course in Miracles* teaches that "perception alone can be distorted." It's only your perception of life's situations that can be inaccurate or mistaken.

This lesson was powerfully reinforced for Dean, a highly educated father who felt hopeless in the challenging circumstances within his family and his inability to let go of his grief. For seven years, Dean had annual telephone readings to support overcoming his dreadful guilt over the tremendous loss of two family members who had taken their own lives.

Suicide has a great deal of stigma and often is described as demonic and damaging to the spirit. The essence of the spirit can never be permanently harmed. Spirit and soul are perfect and holy, but perception can be distorted. It's comforting to know that a spirit's soul is never lost; but the spirit can be temporarily bewildered.

Two main loved ones related to Dean had committed suicide, and his ego-mind wrestled with the anxious, depleting, and unending question of *why?* The ego-mind has a stubborn and inventive way to imprison the survivors of suicide with thoughts like: Why didn't I do more? I should have done this. I could have done that. Why didn't I see this coming?

Stan, Dean's father, had been drafted into the military in his teens against his will. He left a loving relationship and supportive family to survive in a fearful, bloody battlefield for four years. The horrors of war saturated his mind with insecurity and fear, and he suffered from PTSD. Upon returning home from the war, Stan was heartbroken when he learned his wife was leaving him for one of his friends. He tried hard to complete a college education, but his mind was unable to focus. He felt defeated and worked part-time jobs in local factories and turned to alcohol to try to forget the horrible images of war.

His drinking prevented him from getting to visit with his son Dean. Just before Dean graduated high school, he learned that his dad Stan had taken his own life. Dean was told very little about the circumstances of his dad's life, and he often felt ashamed and unloved because he hadn't spent more time with him. During Dean's first reading, some thirty years after his father's passing, Stan communicated the challenging circumstances of his life and the mental demons he had been battling.

Once Dean had more understanding of his dad's trials and had validated the information about his dad with his aunt after the reading, he changed his hopeless perspective about his dad. Dean was reassured to feel he wasn't somehow responsible for his dad's death because he hadn't spent more time with him and that his father loved him dearly.

Also presenting during Dean's readings was a younger male, who first humbly communicated that he was an exceptional artist, then showed me colorful abstract paintings in my mind's eye. I saw him with long, wavy dark hair and a backpack, and he was wearing a blue and white football jersey. I relayed this information to Dean, and he confirmed it was his son Eric. Dean also confirmed that Eric had been majoring in graphic design in college when he passed, but his passion had been oil painting. Intensely, I sensed Eric's uneasiness and sadness just before he passed, and I felt the uncomfortable sense of constriction around my throat, as if I couldn't breathe. With guilt and shame, Dean explained that his son had hung himself before his college graduation.

In my mind, I could see a large reddish-colored dog sitting at

Eric's feet, and Dean was comforted to know Eric's dog Maggie, an Irish setter, had found him on the other side. I also could see Eric and Maggie playing in the water and swimming together.

Over the phone, I could hear Dean weeping as we connected with his son. He told me he couldn't talk about his son with his wife and his mother; they denied the suicide and refused to ever speak of Eric. They had removed his photos and his art while Dean was at work. Dean said he even considered ending his own life. I referred him to a few exceptional grief counselors and several grief organizations.

During the next reading, the following year, Dean received more messages from both his father Stan and his son Eric. Together, these two spirits encouraged Dean to reevaluate the circumstances of his life. Eric showed me his father sitting in a cubicle, alone and isolated at his job. I saw him writing codes, and Dean told me he was a computer programmer and worked mostly alone. In my mind, I saw plaques on the wall for awards, and I saw journals with articles about Dean. Humbly, Dean replied that he had received three major awards for software design and at least a dozen articles had been written about his technological skills.

Stan communicated that although he was very proud of Dean's accomplishments, he was also pleased he was practicing yoga and tai chi and studying Eastern philosophy and meditation. His dad conveyed that he knew Dean felt trapped and unhappy in his work and encouraged him to find his passion. Dean was fascinated that his dad knew he was currently studying Buddhism and yoga, and he acknowledged how unhappy he was with his career.

Eric then wanted to let his dad know he was concerned about his hopelessness with his mom. I received the impression that Dean was still not able to communicate with his wife or mother about Eric's passing and this caused lots of tension. Dean asked if Eric was ever around his mother and grandmother, and if he shared messages with them. Eric shared that neither was open to his presence and didn't recognize the signs he often shared: turtles with his mom and frogs with his grandma.

Dean was surprised that his wife didn't recognize the connection with turtles, because Eric had had several pet turtles growing up, and his bedroom had images of turtles, frogs, and lizards. Eric's grandma Isabel had given him a stuffed frog when he was a little boy, and it was still in his room. Eric asked his father to please encourage these ladies to come to speak with a medium so their hearts could heal. He promised Eric he would share these messages.

Although Dean's energy seemed less heavy with depression and guilt, it still felt as if he didn't value his life or have much enjoyment. He asked me if I knew of any organization focused on helping parents who had lost children to suicide.

Serendipity is the way of spirit, and as I was working with Dean, a client from Canada was gifted with a parallel message from three family members who had taken their lives. Dana had a son, father, and brother in spirit who had tragically committed suicide. As Dean's father and son were helping him, Dana's loved ones in spirit were helping Dana and her soul family learn the value of perspective.

Dana became the president of a chapter of Survivors of Suicide, an organization to help grieving families who had suffered incredible losses, as she had. She healed her own saddened outlook by helping others to release and let go of their guilt and blame. Because of her readings with me at just the right moment, I was able to connect Dean to her organization.

For his third reading, Dean surprised me (and, I'm sure, Eric in spirit) and put his mom Isabel on the phone. At first, Isabel was extremely closed. She was afraid her priest wouldn't approve of communicating with the dead, and her strong religious beliefs were of great concern to her.

Eric communicated that angels were real and he appreciated Grandma Isabel lighting altar candles for his soul. Clairvoyantly, I saw her sewing Eric's First Communion and Confirmation suits, and he wanted grandma to know he missed her meatballs. In my mind, Eric presented an infant wrapped in a pink blanket, and the baby had what looked like a white lacey dress on. Isabel cried and said she had had a daughter who lived only a few days and she buried her in the baptism dress she had sewn for her. Even Dean was stunned because his mom had never spoken about losing a child.

Suddenly, I heard enthusiasm in her voice and she asked how I knew these things. I explained that her grandson was present and communicating with us. Eric also told his grandma he knew if he brought her little girl through, she would believe in their presence.

After several other relatives in spirit communicated with Isabel, she was asked to help Sabrina, her daughter-in-law, to be open to receive messages from her son Eric. Also, Isabel's husband Stan told her he loved her and that Heaven was a very loving place to be. He was aware of her recent diagnosis with her liver and said she would be supported by her family in spirit.

Sometimes spirits disclose circumstances unknown to others. I discovered that Isabel was having abdominal pain and she had just been in the hospital getting lots of tests. The day after her reading, she was diagnosed with liver cancer.

Isabel convinced Sabrina to get a reading so she could release her buried emotions. Even though she was still averse to the idea, Sabrina scheduled an in-person reading. As she sat for her session, she let me know she didn't believe in this hocus pocus, but she wanted to find out how I received all this information.

With my clairaudience, I heard the name Juliet, and she nodded, acknowledging that she knew that name. "Who is Juliet?" I asked. Immediately astonished, Sabrina said it was her real name and Sabrina was her middle name. Her son Eric came through holding paintbrushes and empty canvases. He communicated to encourage his mom to paint again.

Eric then showed me images of his mom with a green shawl, riding in a yellow convertible. On the radio, I could hear Christian rock music, and he showed me his mom driving to a bluff overlooking the ocean, with a lighthouse in the distance. Then I saw paintings of red, white, and blue lighthouses in different sizes.

Sabrina kept biting her lower lip and looking down at the floor. I asked her if this information made sense to her. She was astonished. She had used a different name to schedule the reading so I couldn't do research on her, and she hadn't even told her family, as I had read for her husband and mother-in-law before. She wept for several minutes before she could speak. Every Sunday, instead of going to church, she'd driven her convertible to the Pacific Ocean bluffs and painted lighthouses. Ever since Eric had passed, she'd been unable to paint.

On her last visit to the beach, Sabrina explained she asked God to show her a sign that Eric was all right, and she suddenly came across a baby sea turtle tangled in a fishnet washed up on the beach. As soon as she freed this little creature, she felt the presence of Eric hug her from behind. He communicated that, yes, he'd been there, and he wanted his mom to release herself from the net of shame and guilt in which she was trapped.

Within several days, Dean phoned to acknowledge his gratitude for helping his mom and wife change their perception about the eternity of Eric's soul and the continuity of life.

Our friends in spirit are truly awe-inspiring in their ability to shift our awareness from fear, shame, and guilt to virtue, benevolence, and grace. They act as lighthouses to guide us on our journey, and our shift in perception will bring us Home.

WHAT IT ALL MEANS
FOR YOU

The messages shared in *Lasting Impressions*—both personal and universal—will have unique significance for you depending on your life experiences. Perhaps your consciousness expanded with knowledge of spiritual truths, or perhaps your beliefs were confirmed. You may have realized there's nothing to forgive and you are forgiven. Your sense of loss may have dissipated when you discovered your loved ones are still with you. Or, you may have ceased to worry about them when you learned they are safe and growing in love. On one hand, you may have realized you're satisfied knowing they're with you and you will see them again. On the other hand, you may wish to contact your loved ones in spirit through a medium to obtain a higher perspective on your own life and find out more about their journey.

Spirit communication is magically mysterious! Should you decide to get a reading, remember that the process is managed by your loved ones in spirit, but everyone involved plays an important part. Extraordinary communication occurs when the considerations and intentions of the medium, sitter, and spirit are aligned.

Reliable mediums will blend their consciousness with your loved ones in spirit to present messages with specificity, clarity, and purpose. As the sitter, the more unbiased and easygoing you can be, the greater the likelihood you will appreciate and value your messages. Your openness as well as that of the medium influences the accessibility of the spirit world and spirit's capacity to communicate discernible and profound messages.

The sacred continuity of life and eternal soul connections are the principal reasons for spirit communication, which is genuine and continuous, even if you aren't conscious of it. Imagine how you would live your life if you whole-heartedly trusted that you are an eternal being and you will always be with your loved ones. Equally important, imagine how you would live if you trusted that the eternal essence of each and every being is Love.

Whatever you received by reading *Lasting Impressions,* may it bless you.

ABOUT THE AUTHOR

Since childhood, **Geoffrey Jowett** has had the ability to sense and connect with the unseen world of spirit. It wasn't until later in life, however, that he chose to make a career of spiritual mediumship. First, he cultivated his affinities for the biological sciences and natural law. He obtained a Bachelor of Biology from the State University of New York at Brockport and a Master of Cell and Molecular Biology from the University of Buffalo.

For a decade after college, Geof pursued a career in biotechnology as a molecular biologist, project manager, and biotech instructor. He then followed a unique career path in higher education: first, as a college biology and anatomy instructor at four traditional colleges and universities; then, as dean of students at an art and design college; and finally, as vice president of student affairs at a university of alternative medicine.

Behind the scenes throughout these years, Geof nurtured his interest in spirituality and higher consciousness. He received certification from the Morris Pratt Institute in Mediumship and became an ordained minister through the New Thought Spiritual

Center of Palm Springs. In a stroke of divine serendipity, he was fortunate to grow up just miles from Lily Dale Assembly, the international center of modern spiritualism in upstate New York. Here, he refined and learned to better understand his skill as a spiritual medium and intuitive.

Geof now finds his greatest calling and joy to be communicating messages from the higher vibrational plane of spirit. He also provides readings of individual soul progression and personal Akashic records. In these endeavors, he integrates his logical, scientifically trained mind with his intuition and spiritual insight. For over ten years, he has used his organizational and teaching skills to facilitate workshops in spiritual development, intuition, chakra balancing, meditation, karma, and reincarnation. Linking natural science with spirit is his passion.

Geof is the author and creator of three other books and two meditation CDs, including:

- *The Power of I Am: Aligning the Chakras of Consciousness*
- *What's Cooking in Heaven, Grandma?*
- *Hope for Parents Who Have Lost Children: A Medium's Communication with Children in Heaven*
- *Allowing Peace: Self-Guided Meditations with Your Spirit Guides* (Meditation CD)
- *Harmonizing the Chakras of Consciousness* (Meditation CD)

Through all of his endeavors, Geof helps others on their journeys of enlightenment to recognize that each of us is an eternal and infinite part of God, and that our most important purpose in life is to perpetuate divine love.

It would be Geof's joy and privilege to help you communicate with your loved ones in spirit and better understand your soul's purpose and progress. For more information or to schedule a reading, workshop, or presentation, please see his website or feel free to connect with him.

Geof Jowett, Intuitive Medium
Website: www.geofjowett.com
562-355-0525
Email: geof@geofjowett.com
Facebook: Geoffrey Jowett
Twitter: Mediumgeof
Yelp: Geof Jowett

Made in the USA
Lexington, KY
11 January 2018